ENDORSEMENTS

For generations, much controversy has surrounded a woman's role in the church. In her timely new release, *God's Heart for Women*, Rhonda equips believers with a tool that not only dispels lies of the enemy but reveals the heart of God's divine plan for both men and women.

Grounded in extensive study, Rhonda highlights the foundational truth that both man and woman were intricately crafted in the image and likeness of God—an affirmation echoed by God Himself. In the pages of this book, she skillfully navigates biblical teachings, unveiling God's intentional design for unity between man and woman.

As a friend and fellow woman in ministry, I am honored to recommend *God's Heart for Women* as a transformative guide that will undoubtedly solidify God's profound intention for men and women to stand hand in hand in His divine purpose. Rhonda's work is not just a book; it's a testament to the unity God envisioned for His creation. Prepare to be enlightened and inspired on this journey of understanding God's heart for His children.

Lynette Hagin
Director of Rhema Bible Training College

God's Heart for Women: Empowering Women to Answer His Call in Life & Ministry is a revealing book that will address both theological questions and cultural backgrounds throughout the Old and New Testament about women and their God-given purpose and calling according to Scripture. This book will not only answer questions regarding women and their role in life and ministry that have been perplexing generations, it will help propel women into the destiny that God has purposed for them.

Pastor Rhonda Garver, a well-respected woman who has been in ministry for over 30 years, has eloquently written this book with purpose and intent. The Holy Spirit, through her, unveils within these pages a divine shift from wrong mindsets that have been held for centuries regarding women. She takes you on an in-depth journey of study and dissecting of scripture that will reveal to the reader all that God has desired and planned for women.

I know this book, which has been written from the heart of God, will be a valuable tool of inspiration, transformation, and will be life-altering. It should be required reading for any serious student of the Bible all over the world. Through careful study of these truths, this book will encourage every woman to step into and pursue their God-given call and to never have to question it again.

Dr. Mary Frances Varallo
International Minister and Author
Founder and President of MFVM

It was a pleasure reading Rhonda Garver's work, *God's Heart for Women*. As I reviewed the content, I couldn't help but think of the massive contributions made by women to the Body of Christ over the past 2,000 years, and how impoverished the Church would be without the labors of gifted women who have served selflessly to advance the cause of Christ. Rhonda reminds us of the valiant and notable ministries of biblical women such as Deborah, Huldah, Priscilla, Phoebe, and Junia. Far from being second-class workers, women have historically provided first-class ministry in the Body of Christ, and in a day when the Church needs "all hands on deck," Rhonda's work provides a welcome and encouraging word.

Tony Cooke
Bible Teacher and Author

As I read through this book, I was so blessed that Pastor Rhonda Garver has taken on the task of an in-depth study of God's Word concerning the subject of women preachers. There is much confusion around this hotly debated subject.

We don't need man's ideas about this area, but we need biblical truths. In this book Pastor Rhonda does a deep dive into the Word of God and brings out those truths and they are life changing.

These are the last days and we need every voice, male and female, to preach the uncompromised Word of God!

Trent Cloin
Pastor, Midwest Believers Church

I just read Rhonda Garver's book, *God's Heart for Women*. It is by far the best book I have read on women biblically and women in ministry. Her approach to this subject is in-depth and for all the right reasons. I didn't grow up in the church and didn't realize what an issue this has been for thousands of years. When I became a Christian and then into a local church, it was one where both men and women ministered, and I saw the value of both and in both. When I started to hear that women in ministry were an issue for many, it surprised me. Obviously, there was some misunderstanding. Rhonda's book goes way beyond just the women in ministry question, and as you read it, you will come away with a more complete view of women from the scriptures.

John Grunewald
Rhema International Director for Europe, Africa, and the Middle East
President/Founder Grunewald Ministries

I don't mean it lightly when I say that Rhonda Garver's book *God's Heart for Women* has to be the best book on this subject, or at least the best that I have read. What a powerful book!

The way Rhonda takes you on a journey through the scriptures challenges the reader while delivering insightful truth. I love her heart to not just write from experience, but to show the intention of the Father from the very beginning.

This book is so needed for the Body of Christ and will save a lot of heartache and frustration for many. If you are a man in ministry, you need this book. If you are a woman in ministry, you need this book. If you have a problem with women in ministry, you need this book. If you don't know where you stand on the subject, you need to read this book. Everyone needs to read this book!

Kenneth Estrada
Pastor and Author
Kingdom Life Church

GOD'S HEART FOR WOMEN

Published by Harrison House Publishers
Shippensburg, PA 17257

ISBN 13 TP: 978-1-6675-0953-2
ISBN 13 eBook: 978-1-6675-0954-9

For Worldwide Distribution, Printed in the U.S.A.
1 2 3 4 5 6 7 8 / 29 28 27 26 25

GOD'S HEART
FOR WOMEN

RHONDA GARVER

DEDICATION

This book is dedicated to all of the wonderful, inspiring women of God whom I have had the honor to know throughout my life. Women who have selflessly served God, often at great personal cost and despite formidable obstacles. I have learned from and been inspired by each one of you, from my spiritual mother who I watched daily lay down her life in service to our King, to my wonderful daughter who is just starting out on her faith journey with God; from those who taught me the Word and lived it before me, to those with whom I have been honored to work and minister. Each of you have blessed, inspired, and motivated me to pursue excellence in my service to Him and this book is dedicated to you!

ACKNOWLEDGMENTS

First, I must acknowledge my heavenly Father, Jesus my Savior, and the precious Holy Spirit. For every day of my life, You have been my ever-present and closest friend. I am in awe of Your love, mercy, and grace, which is more than I deserve and for which I am eternally grateful!

I would like to thank my precious husband, Mark. After my own salvation and relationship with God, you are the greatest gift God ever gave me. Thank you for sincerely loving God and sincerely loving me. You have always kept us moving forward in pursuit of the plan of God, and without your support (and occasional push ☺), I don't know when or if this book would have come to be. I am grateful!

I want to thank Chad Hasting for donating His artwork for this book (you can find Chad at three.and.co on Instagram) and Cody Edger for taking the picture on the back of this book.

I would also like to acknowledge all of our wonderful staff and our church family. Thank you! Your love, support, encouragement, and devotion to this plan of God called Cornerstone Word of Life Church is a blessing to me. It is a joy to do life and ministry with you!

CONTENTS

FOREWORD

First, let me say that it is a great privilege to be asked to write the foreword for Rhonda Garver's amazing and enlightening work *God's Heart for Women*. It is, without any doubt in my mind, the most encouraging book I've ever read on the subject of women and their uniqueness, purpose, and value in the eyes of God. As I read each page carefully and meditated on its content, I was so encouraged and admonished by the precious truths that are contained in Scripture and in Rhonda's eloquent explanations, not only of the value of women in ministry, but of the value and treasure that women are to God's heart as a whole.

Rhonda's insights show so gloriously from Scripture that God does not see a distinction between man and woman in their ability to be used by Him—and that He made Adam and Eve as co-rulers. Rhonda also explains the amazing positions of authority into which God placed many women in the Old Testament.

Although Satan has tried so hard through the ages to put women down, when Jesus came, He was the most powerful delivering voice for demonstrating the value of women. From the woman at the well, whom Jesus should not have even been talking to according to the culture of that day, to Mary Magdalene, to whom He appeared first after His resurrection—Jesus revealed a woman's value. And from the gospels to the epistles, Rhonda brings such great revelation on this subject from the writers of Scripture, who were inspired by the Holy Spirit. In particular, Rhonda speaks of the writings of the apostle Paul, where he said that in Christ, there is neither Jew nor Greek, bond nor free, *male* nor *female* (Galatians 3:28).

Dear reader, no matter who you are—a man, a woman, a husband, a wife, a mother, or a father (and maybe you're the mother or father of a little girl)—it is my strongest opinion that we need to see the truth about women from God's point of view in His Holy Scriptures. We all need to see and walk in the light of what God says about each one of us in His Word. But from the beginning in Genesis, God has placed woman in a very elevated, noble position, and this truth has not been largely understood.

Psalm 68:11 is said to be a special Messianic promise—that when you see these things happening, that is, women carrying the Good News *en masse*, it is a sign of the Messiah's soon return. I believe this book by Rhonda Garver not only carries great truth that we need to know and take into our heart and mind, but it presents wonderful teaching to help us better understand the time we're living in.

It is so vitally important that women see themselves and their value through Scripture, not just through tradition carried down to us and embraced by society over the centuries. I write this foreword not only with love and respect for Rhonda Garver, but with the purpose of recommending this crucial teaching so that its truths can be uncovered and embraced for years to come—for the glory of God and His heart's expression of love toward His invaluable creation, *woman*.

Denise Renner
Minister, author, and broadcaster
Moscow, Russia

CHAPTER 1

THE JOURNEY BEGINS

She sat across the desk from me, her shoulders heaving from quiet sobs, her tears streaming through her fingers, which were tightly clasped to her face. "I don't know what to do," she began. "I know with all my heart that God called me to the ministry, but does the Bible really say I can't obey Him?"

I knew this young lady very well. She and her family had been a vital part of our church for a long time.

"What happened," I asked, "to upset you so badly today?"

She is from a smaller town outside of where our church is located, one of those towns where everyone knows everyone. She explained that she had bumped into a few pastors downtown who used to be under her grandfather's oversight in ministry and they had confronted her about some speaking engagements she had accepted. A few small churches in their area had asked her to come and minister and she had accepted those invitations. The meetings had gone well, many people had been ministered to, and the pastors of those churches were thrilled with her ministry. Then she ran into those *other* pastors who were ministers in her small town who didn't believe women should minister and their words to her were very mean and cutting. In fact, they told her that her grandfather, with whom she had been very close before his death, would "roll over in his grave" in horror to hear she had been "ministering." Their words, particularly their assertion that her grandfather, who was her hero, would be horrified with what she was doing, plus the fact that they were insistent God Himself was displeased with her, had cut her heart deeply.

"I don't *ever* want to disobey God *or* His Word. I just don't know what to do!" she cried.

I hugged and comforted her. Then I told her what I knew biblically about the subject of women in ministry at that time. But I also told her I would study the subject more in-depth and get back with her.

Around that same time, a dear friend in ministry contacted me and asked if I could teach on Women and Women in Ministry in a Bible school she operates in another nation. I told her I could probably teach an hour on it, but I didn't think I had the material to teach for the number of hours she was wanting me to teach on this subject. These two incidents coming so close together sent me to the Word for the understanding I needed to help both of them.

In retrospect, it almost seems silly that I hadn't studied this subject in-depth before then. My husband and I had been pastoring together for over 20 years by that time, but I had just never made the subject a big focus of mine. I had studied the Bible on this a little bit and read a few books that looked at the subject, and though those books didn't dig into it as deeply as I wanted, the Word I knew and those books were enough to satisfy me—especially since the call I personally experienced had been so supernatural. But I knew if I was going to help this young lady and others like her, it was going to require a more comprehensive study on the subject. I had to resolve this issue once and for all for myself, this young lady, and all of the other women here and around the world who were stuck in the same quandary as she was.

Let me first begin by saying, I am a stickler for the Word of God. The Bible answers all questions and we go to the Bible to form what we believe. We don't go to the Bible to try and find scriptures to prove what we already believe. We form our beliefs from what the Word says.

I would never twist a scripture to fit what I believe, and in fact, that was my issue with the books I bought to read after my meeting with this young lady. I bought a couple of books on the subject of women in ministry, but I never got very far into them before I quit reading. To me, it felt like they were trying too hard to make the Bible say something they wanted it to say. I just couldn't do it that way.

So, I spent some time in prayer asking the Holy Spirit who inspired the Bible to open unto me the revelation that I needed on this subject, and then I dug into the Word.

But before we even get into the meat of this book, I want to ask you to examine yourself. What do *you* think about women and God's dealings with them when it comes to ministry and leadership in the Body of Christ (the church)? Equally important, who or what formed those beliefs in you? How much time have *you* spent studying these issues in-depth for yourself? Far too many, I believe, just parrot their pastor or church leaders or other people on this issue, and far too few have taken the time to dig into and study on it for themselves.

This is a biblical topic about which few are neutral. When I began to study on this, I was amazed at the noise level out there on these issues. In fact, there are people who are virulently opposed to women in ministry, but they have never studied the Bible in-depth on this subject for themselves.

I know there are a whole lot of really sincere people who believe the Bible genuinely teaches that women are not to minister and they are willing to stand up and defend or fight for what they truly believe the Bible says about women and specifically women in ministry. On one hand, I applaud them for that. We *have to be* sticklers for the Word! If our doctrine is not found in the Word then we ought not be teaching it. I applaud them for their commitment to the veracity of the Word as they understand it. But therein lies the problem, I believe. They have never studied the Bible in-depth themselves on this subject to gain understanding and to develop informed beliefs. They are basing their opinions on the opinions of others or on a cursory reading of the scriptures, and from that cursory or quick and superficial reading of the Word, they have built hard and fast doctrines for which they are more than willing to fight.

I actually understand where they are coming from. If you just skim over the scriptures, I can understand why so many have come to the conclusions that they have.

But a cursory reading of the scriptures is not enough.

What does the Bible actually say on these issues? We need to know!

Study to shew thyself approved unto God, a workman that needeth not to be ashamed, rightly dividing the word of truth (2 Timothy 2:15 KJV).

We are to *study* the scriptures so that we can be approved unto God and be a workman that needeth not to be ashamed. The implied subject in that sentence is *you*. *You study* to show yourself approved and so that *you* can *rightly* divide the word of truth.

Now the Berean Jews were of more noble character than those in Thessalonica, for they received the message with great eagerness and examined the Scriptures every day to see if what Paul said was true (Acts 17:11 NIV).

The Bereans studied every day to make sure what they had heard was true, and because they did, the scriptures say they were of more noble character. It is not only our right and our privilege to study the Word of God, it is our *responsibility* to do so, especially if you are a teacher of it.

Not many of you should become teachers, my fellow believers, because you know that we who teach will be judged more strictly (James 3:1 NIV).

If you are a teacher or preacher of the Word then this scripture says we will be judged more strictly. It is your *responsibility* to study and get it right! Therefore, we cannot just parrot what someone else has said. We cannot just skim over the surface of the scriptures, but we are to *study* so that we can get it right!

I knew a cursory or surface reading of the scriptures wasn't going to be enough. I saw what is on the surface in the scriptures, I heard the sermons people have taught over the years, but I also knew that there were a lot of women in the Bible whom God called and used to speak for Him, and He used them to lead both naturally and spiritually.

I know a lot of women in church history and in our day with supernatural callings from God to preach and teach and lead; so, how can we explain God anointing women to preach and teach as outlined in the Bible if He truly didn't want them to do it? Would God anoint something He is against?

So many women throughout church history have been used by God to bring revival to the church, to bring repentance to the sinner, to work miracles and administer healing in the name of Jesus, and to even change whole nations in His name.

So, how do you reconcile the beliefs of many with the actions of *God* Himself that we see through women, especially those in the Bible?

It all comes down to the Word (the Bible)! What does the Word of God truly say about women and women in ministry when you really study it out?

We are about to find out.

Everything we say and do *has* to be scriptural, and for something to be scriptural it has to be found in scripture. I know that should be obvious but it is amazing to me how often people seem to forget that.

So, that is where we are going to go, to the scriptures. No one's experience and no one's opinion is good enough if their experience and opinions do not match up with the Word of God. The following pages are what I discovered about God's dealings with women from the beginning when I began to study and the Holy Spirit began unfolding the Word of God to me on this subject.

If what you find in the Word disagrees with something you have been taught, then I adjure you before God to study it for yourself and see what the Bible, the Word of God, actually says. We have a responsibility to get it right.

In this book, I have intentionally chosen not to delve into the subject of marriage and the relationship between husbands and wives. The Bible has a lot to say about that, but I chose not to try and tackle that in this book as it is far too vast a subject and I wanted to keep the content of this book sharp and on point as to God's heart and purpose for women. Perhaps that will be another book for another day.

I hope the truths from the Word of God that are unfolded in the following chapters will mean as much to you as they do to me as the Holy Spirit took me on a tour of the Word and showed me the Father's dealings with women and the heart and plan of God when it comes to women.

CHAPTER 2

IN THE BEGINNING

So, where do we begin? At the beginning, the book of Genesis.

I decided to do a linear study of the Word of God on the subject of women starting in Genesis. I want us first to see what was in the heart and mind of God concerning men and women when He created us. The first few chapters of the Bible give us God's original design for humanity, for both men and women. We find here what God created us to do and be *before the fall*, before Satan got in there and messed it all up!

So, let's dig in and see what was His original plan.

I want us to look at every time that humans are mentioned in the first few chapters of the book of Genesis in the Bible, the chapters before the fall, and see what God says about us.

Genesis 1:26 is the first time humans are mentioned in the Bible.

And God said, Let us make man in our image, after our likeness: and let them have dominion over the fish of the sea, and over the fowl of the air, and over the cattle, and over all the earth, and over every creeping thing that creepeth upon the earth (Genesis 1:26 KJV).

When God said, "Let Us make man in Our image…and let them have dominion," exactly who was He talking about—"man" as in males or "man" as in mankind, which would include both males and females? Because the King James Version uses the word *man*, the assumption may be that God is talking about males, but is He?

I looked at this scripture in the Interlinear Bible, which is a word for word rendering of the Hebrew into English. In the interlinear verse below, there is the actual Hebrew on the top line, the English translation on the next line, the Strong's concordance number for each word on the next line and the transliteration (or how the Hebrew word would be with our English letters) on the bottom line. Hebrew is read right to left. I put it in here so you could see it with your own eyes.

וַיֹּאמֶר ²⁶	אֱלֹהִים	נַעֲשֶׂה	אָדָם	בְּצַלְמֵנוּ	כְּדְמוּתֵנוּ	וְיִרְדּוּ
And said,	God	Let us make	man	in our image,	after our likeness:	and let them have dominion
559	430	6213	120	6754	1823	7287
Wayo'mer	'Elohiym	Na'"seh	'aadaam	b'tsalmeenuw	kidmuwteenuw	w'yirduw

בִדְגַת	הַיָּם	וּבְעוֹף	הַשָּׁמַיִם	וּבַבְּהֵמָה	וּבְכָל	הָאָרֶץ
over the fish of	the sea,	and over the fowl of	the air,	and over the cattle,	and over all	the earth,
1710	3220	5775	8064	929	3605	776
bidgat	hayaam	uwb'owp	hashaamayim	uwbab'heemaah	uwbkaal-	haa'aarets

וּבְכָל	הָרֶמֶשׂ	הָרֹמֵשׂ	עַל	הָאָרֶץ:
and over every	creeping thing	that creepeth	upon	the earth.
3605	7431	7430	5921	776
uwbkaal-	haaremes	haaromees	'al-	haa'aarets

That word translated "man" in verse 26 is the Hebrew word *aadaam* (Adam), pronounced Ah-Dahm, which is the Hebrew word for "human being" or "mankind as a whole." (See Appendix A for more details.) When the Godhead called him Adam in this verse, They were calling him Mankind or Human, which is what the word *Adam* actually means in Hebrew. It is not so much a particular man's name as it is a designation of species.

This verse literally says, "Let Us make mankind in Our image, after Our likeness: and let them, mankind, have dominion."

Some of the more modern versions bring this out.

God said, Let Us [Father, Son, and Holy Spirit] make mankind in Our image, after Our likeness, and let them have complete authority over the fish of the sea, the birds of the air, the [tame] beasts, and over all of the earth, and over everything that creeps upon the earth (Genesis 1:26 AMPC).

Then God said, "Let us make mankind in our image, in our likeness, so that they may rule over the fish in the sea and the birds in the sky, over the livestock and all the wild animals, and over all the creatures that move along the ground" (Genesis 1:26 NIV).

It really is unfortunate that the King James Version translated *Adam* as "man" instead of "mankind" because this version of the Bible is read by so many people. In so many people's minds, it puts women in a deficit from the very first verse about humanity in the Bible. This verse is not referring to just males being created in the image and likeness of God and being given authority over the earth, but He was talking about all human beings, mankind, both male and female being created in His image and in His likeness and being given authority together.

The next verse, Genesis 1:27, clarifies it even further.

So God created man [Hebrew: Adam, meaning human beings or mankind] in his own image, in the image of God created he him; male and female created he them (Genesis 1:27 KJV).

11

It says, "in the image of God created he him." The word *him* is not in the original language of this verse. My interlinear says the word in Hebrew they translated "him" is an untranslatable mark of the accusative case. It is an untranslatable mark that has nothing to do with being male.

אֹתֹו	בָּרָא	אֱלֹהִים	בְּצֶלֶם	בְּצַלְמֹו	הָאָדָם	אֵת	אֱלֹהִים	וַיִּבְרָא ²⁷
him;	created he	God	in the image of	in his own image,	man		God	So created
853	1254	430	6754	6754	120	853	430	1254
'otow	baaraa'	'Elohiym	b'tselem	b'tsalmow	haa'aadaam	'et-	'Elohiym	Wayibraa'

אֹתָם:	בָּרָא	וּנְקֵבָה	זָכָר
them.	created he	and female	male
853	1254	5347	2145
'otaam	baaraa'	uwnqeebaah	zaakaar

Men and women both were created in the image and likeness of God. God goes out of His way to say so, so that there would be no confusion about it, and then He goes on to reiterate in the next verse that He gave humanity of both sexes rulership and dominion over the earth.

And God blessed them, and God said unto them, Be fruitful, and multiply, and replenish the earth, and subdue it: and have dominion over the fish of the sea, and over the fowl of the air, and over every living thing that moveth upon the earth (Genesis 1:28 KJV).

Verse 28 says, "God blessed *them*, and God said unto *them*," plural, meaning both of them "subdue [the earth]: and have dominion."

Both of them, male and female, were given authority and dominion over the earth and every living thing that moveth upon it.

								²⁸
וּמִלְאוּ	וּרְבוּ	פְּרוּ	אֱלֹהִים	לָהֶם	וַיֹּאמֶר	אֱלֹהִים	אֹתָם	וַיְבָרֶךְ
and replenish	and multiply,	Be fruitful,	God	unto them,	and said	God	them,	And blessed
4390	7235	6509	430	3807a	559	430	853	1288
uwmilʾuw	uwrbuw	Pᵉruw	ʾElohiym	laahem	Wayoʾmer	ʾElohiym	ʾotaam	Wayᵉbaarek

הַשָּׁמַיִם	וּבְעוֹף	הַיָּם	בִדְגַת	וּרְדוּ	וְכִבְשֻׁהָ	הָאָרֶץ	אֵת
the air,	and over the fowl of	the sea,	over the fish of	and have dominion	and subdue it:	the earth,	
8064	5775	3220	1710	7287	3533	776	853
hashaamayim	uwbᵉʿowp	hayaam	bidgat	uwrduw	wᵉkibshuhaa	haaʾarets	ʾet-

הָאָרֶץ:	עַל	הָרֹמֶשֶׂת	חַיָּה	וּבְכָל
the earth.	upon	that moveth	living thing	and over every
776	5921	7430	2416	3605
haaʾarets	ʿal-	haaromeset	chayaah	uwbkaal-

The next time humans are mentioned is in Chapter 2.

And every plant of the field before it was in the earth, and every herb of the field before it grew: for the Lord God had not caused it to rain upon the earth, and there was not a man [Hebrew: *Adam,* meaning human beings or mankind] *to till the ground (Genesis 2:5 KJV).*

									⁵
טֶרֶם	הַשָּׂדֶה	עֶשֶׂב	וְכָל	בָאָרֶץ	יִהְיֶה	טֶרֶם	הַשָּׂדֶה	שִׂיחַ	וְכֹל
before	the field	herb of	and every	in the earth,	it was	before	the field	plant of	And every
2962	7704	6212	3605	776	1961	2962	7704	7880	3605
Terem	hasaadeh	ʿeeseb	wᵉkaal-	baaʾarets	yihᵉyeh	Terem	hasaadeh	siyach	Wᵉkol

אַיִן	וְאָדָם	הָאָרֶץ	עַל	אֱלֹהִים	יְהוָה	הִמְטִיר	לֹא	כִּי	יִצְמָח
there was not	and a man	the earth,	upon	God	the Lord	had caused it to rain	not	for	it grew:
369	120	776	5921	430	3068	4305	3808	3588	6779
ʾayin	wᵉʾaadaam	haaʾaarets	ʿal-	ʾElohiym	Yahweh	himTiyr	loʾ	kiy	yitsmaach

הָאֲדָמָה:	אֵת	לַעֲבֹד
the ground.		to till
127	853	5647
haaᵃdaamaah	ʾet-	laᶜᵃbod

But there went up a mist from the earth, and watered the whole face of the ground (Genesis 2:6 KJV).

									⁶
הָאֲדָמָה:	פְּנֵי	כָּל	אֵת	וְהִשְׁקָה	הָאָרֶץ	מִן	יַעֲלֶה	וְאֵד
the ground.	face of	whole	the	and watered	the earth,	from	there went up	But a mist
127	6440	3605	853	9999	8248	776	4480	5927	108
haaᵃdaamaah	pᵉneey-	kaal-	ʾet-	wᵉhishqaah	haaʾarets	min-	yaᶜᵃleh	Wᵉʾeed

13

And the Lord God formed man [Hebrew: *Adam*, meaning human beings or mankind] *of the dust of the ground, and breathed into his nostrils the breath of life; and man* [Hebrew: *Adam*, meaning human beings or mankind] *became a living soul (Genesis 2:7 KJV).*

וַיִּפַּח	הָאֲדָמָה	מִן	עָפָר		הָאָדָם	אֵת	אֱלֹהִים	יְהוָה	וַיִּיצֶר
and breathed	the ground,	of	the dust	of	man		God	the Lord	And formed
5301	127	4480	6083	9999	120	853	430	3068	3335
wayipach	haa''daamaah	min-	'aapaar		haa'aadaam	'et-	'Elohiym	Yahweh	Wayiytser

חַיָּה	לְנֶפֶשׁ	הָאָדָם	וַיְהִי	חַיִּים	נִשְׁמַת	בְּאַפָּיו
living	a soul.	and man	became	life;	the breath of	into his nostrils
2416	5315	120	1961	2416	5397	639
chayaah	l'nepesh	haa'aadaam	Way'hiy	chayiym	nishmat	b''apaayw

That word *his* as in "his nostrils" in verse 7 is not in the original language. The word translated there "his nostrils" is just *nostrils* in the Hebrew without gender specification.

Also, I want you to notice (for future reference) that the first time the word *of* is in this verse, it has a Strong's number of 9999. Anytime you see a 9999 for the Strong's Concordance number it means that word is not in the original language of that verse but that the word was added by the translators for "clarity." In this verse, I think the added 9999 word is of little significance, but in other verses we will look at later, it is hugely significant that the translators added words that were not in the original Hebrew text (or Greek, for the New Testament).

I love verse 7. To me, it so wonderfully reveals the heart of God for the human beings He was creating. It says God *formed* them of the dust of the ground. God used His own hands to "form" us humans from the dust of the ground, like a potter squeezing or pressing the clay into the form He desired. God wanted to be "hands on" when He created mankind. I believe God couldn't wait to get His hands on us!

And the Lord God planted a garden eastward in Eden; and there he put the man [Hebrew: *Adam,* meaning human being or mankind] *whom he had formed (Genesis 2:8 KJV).*

הָאָדָם	אֵת	שָׁם	וַיָּשֶׂם	מִקֶּדֶם	בְּעֵדֶן	גַּן	אֱלֹהִים	יְהוָה	וַיִּטַּע
the man		there	and he put	eastward	in Eden;	a garden	God	the Lord	And planted
120	853	8033	7760	6924	5731	1588	430	3068	5193
haaʾaadaam	ʾet-	shaam	Wayaasem	miqedem	bᵊ-ʿEeden	gan-	ʾElohiym	Yahweh	WayiTaʿ

יָצָר:	אֲשֶׁר
he had formed.	whom
3335	834
yaatsaar	ʾᵃsher

You may be asking, "Why are you making the point that God was referring to mankind as a whole, both genders, when it was obviously just Adam who was created at this point in time?"

Because Eve was still within Adam in these verses! He was talking about both of them, because the two are still one. From the very first verse about humanity in the Bible (Genesis 1:26–28), when God first spoke of creating humans, he referred to them in the plural. They were both contained in that one originally created body until God later separated them. Also, the word that God is using here to refer to Adam literally means human beings or mankind as a whole.

The next time we see humans mentioned is in Genesis 2:15.

And the Lord God took the man [*Adam,* meaning human beings or mankind], *and put him* [that word *him* is not in the Hebrew. It literally just says *put*] *into the garden of Eden to dress it and to keep it (Genesis 2:15 KJV).*

וַיִּקַּח	יְהוָה	אֱלֹהִים	אֶת	הָאָדָם	וַיַּנִּחֵהוּ	בְגַן	עֵדֶן	[15]
And took	the Lord	God		the man,	and put him	into the garden of	Eden	
3947	3068	430	853	120	3240	1588	5731	
Wayiqach	Yahweh	'Elohiym	'et-	haa'aadaam	wayanicheehuw	b'gan-	'Eeden	

לְעָבְדָה	וּלְשָׁמְרָה:
to dress it	and to keep it.
5647	8104
l"aabdaah	uwlshaam'raah

And the Lord God commanded the man [Adam, meaning human beings or mankind], saying, Of every tree of the garden thou mayest freely eat (Genesis 2:16 KJV).

וַיְצַו	יְהוָה	אֱלֹהִים	עַל	הָאָדָם	לֵאמֹר	מִכֹּל	עֵץ	הַגָּן	[16]
And commanded	the Lord	God		the man,	saying,	Of every	tree of	the garden	
6680	3068	430	5921	120	559	3605	6086	1588	
Way'tsaw	Yahweh	'Elohiym	'al-	haa'aadaam	lee'mor	mikol	'eets-	hagaan	

אָכֹל	תֹּאכֵל:
thou mayest freely	eat:
398	398
'aakol	to'keel

But of the tree of the knowledge of good and evil, thou shalt not eat of it: for in the day that thou eatest thereof thou shalt surely die (Genesis 2:17 KJV).

כִּי	מִמֶּנּוּ	תֹּאכֵל	לֹא	וָרָע	טוֹב	הַדַּעַת	וּמֵעֵץ	[17]
for	of it:	thou shalt eat	not	and evil,	good	the knowledge of	But of the tree of	
3588	4480	398	3808	7451	2896	1847	6086	
kiy	mimenuw	to'kal	lo'	waaraa'	Towb	hada'at	Uwmee'eets	

תָּמוּת:	מוֹת	מִמֶּנּוּ	אֲכָלְךָ	בְּיוֹם
die.	thou shalt surely	thereof	thou eatest	in the day that
4191	4191	4480	398	3117
taamuwt	mowt	mimenuw	'akaalkaa	b'yowm

And the Lord God said, It is not good that the man [Adam, meaning human beings or mankind] should be alone; I will make him an help meet for him (Genesis 2:18 KJV).

Neither of the words *him* in this verse are in the Hebrew nor in the meaning of the words they modify.

לְבַדּו	הָאָדָם		הֱיוֹת	טוֹב	לֹא		אֱלֹהִים	יְהוָה	וַיֹּאמֶר
alone;	the man	that	should be	good	not	It is	God	the Lord	And said,
905	120	9999	1961	2896	3808	9999	430	3068	559
l'badow	haa'adaam		h'yowt	Towb	Lo'-		'Elohiym	Yahweh	Wayo'mer

כְּנֶגְדּו:	עֵזֶר	לּו	אֶעֱשֶׂה
meet	an help	for him.	I will make him
5048	5828	3807a	6213
k'neg'dow	'eezer	low	'e''seh-

Here in verse 18, I think the word *help*, or *helper* in some translations, has greatly influenced the opinions of men on the role of women and has influenced many women in how they see themselves and what they were meant to be. So, let's take a closer look at that word.

In our modern vocabulary, when we use the word *helper* we think of someone who is a less skilled assistant, someone who might hand tools to a more skilled person who was working, for instance. But that mental picture is not true to what the scripture is saying here.

The word translated "help" or "helper" in this verse is the Hebrew word *eezer*. That word *eezer* means to aid or to help.

That Hebrew word *eezer* is used 21 times in the Old Testament. Two times, it refers to Eve here in Genesis 2. Three times it refers to people or nations that Israel called on for help when they were under siege, like "Come help us!" or "Come rescue us!" The other 16 times this word refers to God Himself as our helper. He Himself comes to help or rescue us when we are unable to help ourselves. God refers to Himself as *our Eezer*.

Let's break that down. Three times the word translated "help" or "helper" here refers to people or nations that Israel called upon for help when they were under siege. When Israel was under siege and needing to be rescued, they wouldn't call on an inferior people to rescue them if they couldn't rescue themselves. Why would you go to someone weaker or less powerful than you to rescue you from someone more powerful than you? You wouldn't. So, the thought that the one helping was inferior or "less than" the one needing help is just not true to the meaning of this word and its usage in the Old Testament.

Further, since the *majority* of the time when this word for "help" or "helper" was used, 16 out of 21 times in the Old Testament, this word refers to *God* Himself as our helper, then there is no way we could say that the one who was helping was inferior or subordinate to the one being helped. God Himself is certainly not in any way less skilled, inferior, or subordinate to His creation. We would never dream of saying or even thinking that He is.

I want to let that sink in for a moment. The very first word that God uses to describe a woman is a word He uses to describe Himself! Wow! Amazing! We need to change the preconceived ideas in our own thinking that this word translated "help" or "helper" means a woman is inferior or "less than" the man being helped. It simply is not true to the word's meaning and usage in the Old Testament and what this verse of scripture is saying.

So, the woman was removed from the man and brought to him as a separate being (Genesis 2:21-22), not because he needed an inferior, subordinate assistant, but because he needed a counterpart, another one like himself with whom he could fellowship and work and mate. This idea is further brought out by the word after *eezer* in the original text.

In Genesis 1:18 in the King James Version it says "an help meet"—an *eezer k'negdow* in the Hebrew.

That word translated "meet" here in Genesis 2:18 is *k'negdow*, which is word OT:5048 in the Strong's Concordance and its definition is as follows:

> from OT:5046; i.e. part opposite; specifically a counterpart, or mate, usually (adverbial, especially with preposition) over against or before.

For further clarity I went to the word at OT:5046 from which our word is taken as it helps to explain the word used in this verse.

OT:5046 *nagad* a primitive root, properly, to front, i.e. stand boldly out opposite.

To front—to stand boldly out opposite.

Let's look again at the definition of the word translated "meet," *k'negdow*.

K'negdow OT:5048 from *neged* OT:5046; i.e. part opposite; specifically a counterpart, or mate, usually (adverbial, especially with preposition) over against or before.

Eve was pulled out of Adam to stand in front of him, to stand boldly out opposite to him, to be a counterpart or mate.

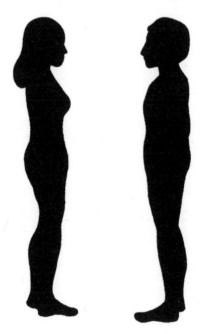

The Young's Literal Translation has this verse this way:

And Jehovah God saith, "Not good for the man to be alone, I do make to him an helper—as his counterpart" (Genesis 2:18 YLT).

Both the Strong's definition of the word *meet* in the King James Version and the Young's Literal Translation calls Eve Adam's counterpart.

Merriam Webster's dictionary app on my phone defines *counterpart* this way:

1: One of two corresponding copies of a legal document: DUPLICATE

2a: A thing that fits another thing perfectly

2b: Something that completes: *complement*

According to the same dictionary app on my phone, the word *complement* means, "something that fills up, completes or makes better or perfect or one of two mutually completing parts."

God made woman as a duplicate copy, which fits the man perfectly. We are mutually completing parts of one another! I love that!

The definition of *counterpart* goes on to say:

3a: one remarkably similar to another

3b: one having the same function or characteristics as another

They both have the same function and characteristics.

Women were *not* created to be an inferior assistant to the man, but to stand face to face, together, one in substance, one in function, hand in hand, ruling and reigning together.

This brings to my mind a mental picture of a man and woman facing each other with arms raised, holding hands with the earth between them, giving a beautiful picture of them as counterparts, both of them created in the image and likeness of God and both having been given authority over the earth.

When God created everything in creation, He said it was good. After mankind was created and everything was done, God said it was very good. Here in verse 18 is the very first time God said something in what He just created was *not good* at least as far as what is recorded in the Bible.

There was something about mankind being alone together, in one body, that was not good for *them*. And I am saying *them* because they were both in there, and when God said it was not good that the man be alone, He used the word *Adam*, which means mankind not just the male. It wasn't good for mankind or human beings to be alone. Woman wasn't created separate from man just to be his mate, like God created male and female cattle. No. He divided the two from one, so each of them could have companionship with the other and so they together would have the ability to make a family and yet they could still be the same in substance and in worth.

Let's read on.

And out of the ground the Lord God formed every beast of the field, and every fowl of the air; and brought them unto Adam [Hebrew: *Adam,* meaning human beings or mankind] *to see what he* [that word *he* is not in the Hebrew] *would call them: and whatsoever Adam* [human beings or mankind] *called every living creature, that was the name thereof. And Adam* [human beings or mankind] *gave names to all cattle, and to the fowl of the air, and to every beast of the field; but for Adam* [human beings or mankind] *there was not found an help meet* [eezer k'negdow] *for him* [that word *him* is not in the Hebrew]. *And the Lord God caused a deep sleep to fall upon Adam* [human beings or mankind] *and he* [that word *he* is not in the Hebrew] *slept: and he took one of his* [that word *his* is not in the Hebrew] *ribs, and closed up the flesh thereof, and the rib, which the Lord God had taken from man* [human beings or mankind], *made he a woman, and brought her unto the man (Genesis 2:19-22 KJV).*

Here in Genesis 2:22 is the first verse in the Bible to differentiate between male and female when referring specifically to human beings—to Adam and his now counterpart Eve. In this verse, the removed part of Adam that God made into the woman is called *ishshah* or "the woman." The male alone is called *ish* in the Hebrew and the woman alone is called *ishshah*.

In this verse the word for "rib" is the Hebrew word *tsela,* which means "a rib, literally (of the body)…a side literally (of a person)." So God may have fashioned Eve from just one rib, but He also may have taken more from Adam up to one entire side to get Eve, so that of the one He could make two.

And Adam said, This is now bone of my bones, and flesh of my flesh: she shall be called Woman, because **she was taken out of Man** *(Genesis 2:23 KJV).*

This separation of the two from one brought them companionship and the ability to reproduce.

This is so interesting to me because when God created the animals, He created both a male and a female. He *created* them separately from their first day. He could have done that with mankind too, but He didn't. He created them together in one body. Then when He saw it wasn't good for there to be just one human, He chose to take part of the one human, Adam, and God fashioned it into a female, a counterpart named Eve. God fashioned the male of what remained and the male part kept the name Adam. He divided Adam, or "the human," and of the one made two, so that she would be the same as Adam only separate from him now. She was before him now, face to face, bone of his bone, flesh of his flesh. Obviously, the flesh and bone are fashioned differently in men and women to facilitate reproduction, but they are of the same substance.

I think this fact makes what God said about marriage in the next few verses come alive to us. Let's read on.

Therefore shall a man leave his father and his mother, and shall cleave unto his wife: and they shall be one flesh. And they were both naked, the man and his wife, and were not ashamed (Genesis 2:24-25 KJV).

This is so fascinating to me. God is such a God of faith. He sees ahead and He established the precedent with humanity of a man leaving his father and his mother, and cleaving unto his wife, before there ever was a father and a mother to leave. Neither Adam nor Eve had a father or a mother, nor were they yet a father and mother themselves. So, God established Adam and Eve as the first family and gave instructions for all the families, all the husbands and wives, who would come after them. Fascinating!

Then God went on to say that the two shall be one flesh. The act of marriage, marital sexual relations, is a putting back together of the two into one. When you are joined together in the act of marriage, the two become one again like it was in the garden. One again in a different way than what they were in the garden, but one again nonetheless.

I also think it is no mistake that humans are one of the only species to mate face to face, facing each other. All of the animals, except one species of chimps, do *not* mate face to face, but humans do. This further illustrates them as counterparts being face to face the way the Bible describes Eve as she was pulled from Adam.

More of this...

...but in a different way. It is the putting back together of the two into one, a visual illustration of how it was in the garden before the fall. A statement of their oneness before God and in His eyes. They are different in form but the same in substance and in purpose.

CHAPTER 3

BUT WHAT ABOUT...?

If women and men are in fact the same in substance and purpose, why then have women been traditionally considered lower than men? Let's look at some of the things people have said about this.

1. ADAM WAS PUT IN CHARGE OF THE GARDEN, MEANING HE WAS PUT AS THE BOSS.

But was he?

> God said, Let Us [Father, Son, and Holy Spirit] make man-kind in Our image, after Our likeness, and let them have complete authority over the fish of the sea, the birds of the air, the [tame] beasts, and over all of the earth, and over everything that creeps upon the earth. So God created man in His own image, in the image and likeness of God He created him; male and female He created them. And God blessed them and said to them, Be fruitful, multiply, and fill the earth, and subdue it [using all its vast resources in the service of God and man]; and have dominion over the fish of the sea, the birds of the air, and over every living creature that moves upon the earth (Genesis 1:26-28 AMPC).

They together, mankind, human beings were given authority in the earth. Adam and Eve were still one here. Both were given authority and dominion.

And the Lord God took the man [Adam, meaning human beings or mankind], and put him [that word him is not in the Hebrew] into the garden of Eden to dress it and to keep it (Genesis 2:15 KJV).

Eve was still in Adam at this point. Mankind or the one human being was put in the garden of Eden to dress and keep it. Not just the male, but *Adam* or mankind.

What else have I heard people say?

2. THE WOMAN WAS CREATED SECOND; THEREFORE, SHE IS LOWER IN RANK AND SUBORDINATE.

But was she?

No. They were created together. If we took that argument—that whoever was created first is greater than and highest in authority and dominion—then any animal God created is greater than and has authority over all mankind, because *they*, the animals, were created before humans were. If you stick with the argument that creation order equals rank, then every human is lower in rank and should be subordinate to frogs because the frogs were created first. But none of us believes that!

We know from our study of the Word so far that Eve was not created second, but they were created together at the same time, both of them in one body. When God formed mankind of the dust of the ground, Eve was made in Adam. They were created together at the same time; that one human being was just later divided into two.

There is a candy bar advertising campaign out right now where they are creating an argument as to which side of their candy bar is better, the right side or the left side. But it is a joke and not a serious question as they are obviously the same. They were made together at the same time and made from the same batch of cookie dough, the same vat of caramel, and the exact same chocolate. One can't be better than the other if they were made at the exact same time, from the exact same things; thus it becomes a silly, laughable advertising campaign. But that is what we do with women and men. Which is better, men or women? Neither! They were made together at the same time, of the same thing, they just got separated later.

If I opened one of those candy bars, took it out of its wrapper, and separated it into two pieces, a left side and a right side, would one piece be better than the other? No! They were still created at the same time from the same things. I can separate the two sides when I open the package, but they are still the same thing, just separated now.

I am not saying that all humans are *exactly* the same and thus interchangeable one for another. I do not mean that there are not distinct differences between the man and the woman. There are distinct physical differences between the two as man and woman, but they are one in substance and one in worth. One is not less than or greater than the other.

What else have people said?

3. WOMAN WAS CREATED AS MAN'S HELPER AND HELPERS ARE INFERIOR AND SUBORDINATE.

Not when you understand what those words mean. See Chapter 2, where we studied what those words actually mean. She wasn't a helper like an inferior assistant, but it has more of the implication of her being a warrior by his side, fighting for him and with him. The modern use of that word has hindered us from seeing what God was actually saying and what He meant when He called Eve Adam's helper. Please refer to Chapter 2 for an in-depth study on those words.

Another thing people have said:

4. THE SERPENT TEMPTED THE WOMAN BECAUSE SHE WAS MORE PRONE TO SIN AND ERROR; THEREFORE, SHE IS INFERIOR.

Let's look at that.

> Now the serpent was more subtil than any beast of the field which the Lord God had made. And he said unto the woman, Yea, hath God said, Ye shall not eat of every tree of the garden? And the woman said unto the serpent, We may eat of the fruit of the trees of the garden: but of the fruit of the tree which is in the midst of the garden, God hath said, Ye shall not eat of it, neither shall ye touch it, lest ye die. And the serpent said unto the woman, Ye shall not surely die: for God doth know that in the day ye eat thereof, then your eyes shall

be opened, and ye shall be as gods, knowing good and evil. And when the woman saw that the tree was good for food, and that it was pleasant to the eyes, and a tree to be desired to make one wise, she took of the fruit thereof, and did eat, and gave also unto her husband with her; and he did eat (Genesis 3:1-6 KJV).

Let's pause here for a moment. While the snake was talking to Eve, where was Adam? This verse says she gave also unto her husband *with* her. He was right there with her when all of this was happening and apparently said or did nothing.

And the eyes of them both were opened, and they knew that they were naked; and they sewed fig leaves together, and made themselves aprons. And they heard the voice of the Lord God walking in the garden in the cool of the day: and Adam and his wife hid themselves from the presence of the Lord God amongst the trees of the garden. And the Lord God called unto Adam, and said unto him, Where art thou? And he said, I heard thy voice in the garden, and I was afraid, because I was naked; and I hid myself. And he said, Who told thee that thou wast naked? Hast thou eaten of the tree, whereof I commanded thee that thou shouldest not eat? And the man said, The woman whom thou gavest to be with me, she gave me of the tree, and I did eat. And the Lord God said unto the woman, What is this that thou hast done? And the woman said, The serpent beguiled me, and I did eat (Genesis 3:7-13 KJV).

The King James Version says that Eve said the serpent beguiled her. That word *beguile*, according to my Merriam-Webster

dictionary app, means "to hoodwink...to lead away by decep-
tion...to deceive by wiles."

Most modern versions say the serpent deceived her. So, Eve
was deceived or tricked by the snake into eating the fruit. But it
doesn't say Adam was deceived. In fact, Adam did not use that as
his defense at all. So, if Adam was not deceived, but he just will-
fully chose to disobey God, how does that make him superior or
better than the woman? At least she was deceived; he just *chose* to
disobey God, fully understanding what he was doing. How does
that make him better than Eve?

CHAPTER 4

AFTER THE FALL

I know the Bible is not a big enough book to contain all that we would like to know, but I would love to have had some documentation of what everyday life was like for Adam and Eve before the fall. I would like to know how they interacted with each other and worked together to exercise their authority and dominion in the earth before Satan got in there and messed it all up!

But we know that they fell and God came to see them anyway and this is what God said to Eve.

To the woman He said, I will greatly multiply your grief and your suffering in pregnancy and the pangs of childbearing; with spasms of distress you will bring forth children. Yet your desire and craving will be for your husband, and he will rule over you (Genesis 3:16 AMPC).

The New Living Translation says it differently and has caused confusion.

Then he said to the woman, "I will sharpen the pain of your pregnancy, and in pain you will give birth. And you will desire to control your husband, but he will rule over you" (Genesis 3:16 NLT).

The New Living Translation is the only version I have seen that translates that phrase as the woman "will desire to control her husband."

In fact, there is a footnote in the New Living Translation that says, "3:16 ★ Or And though you will have desire for your husband / he will rule over you."

Even in their translation or paraphrase, they gave an alternate translation. I have looked at the interlinear, the Young's Literal Translation, as well as a number of other versions and I don't see where they got the word *control* from, but I did want to mention it as sometimes people bring that up. I don't see it anywhere else except in the New Living Translation and even they gave an alternate translation. Since the New Living Translation is the only version I know that says anything like that and even they give an alternate translation, I see no corroborating evidence that is the correct interpretation.

I do want you to note that God said it was a woman's husband who would rule over her. It does *not* say all men would rule over all women.

Some men, due to their own now-fallen nature, have decided that they are free to abuse and mistreat women. Of course, that is not true of *all* men, but there are far too many men around the world who feel that way.

In India, from ancient times until it was outlawed by the British, living widows would be tied to their dead husband's body and as they burned his dead body, they would burn her alive so she could "serve him in the afterlife."

I heard a news story about a woman in Saudi Arabia who said that by law, a male relative must control a woman's life from birth to death, effectively treating all women as permanent legal minors. I heard of one woman who had to have her 15-year-old son sign off on legal papers so she could travel.

Women are widely regarded as property in some parts of the world.

In some countries, men who physically abuse, maim, or even kill women are not prosecuted.

In some countries, little girls are forced into prostitution or sold to older adult men to be their "wives" at seven or eight years old.

When it comes to the consequences of the fall, *this is **not** what God intended!* It is contrary to His character and nature! All of this is a result of humanity's now-fallen nature and the enemy getting in here and twisting and perverting what God intended for men and women to be.

I believe that we, as the church of the Living God, can and should live as close to God's original purpose as possible and we should not on *any* level yield to the enemy's perversion of our roles and relationships and responsibilities one to another!

The Bible has to be the final word on these matters.

God knew what He said and what He meant when He told Adam and Eve what would happen as a result of the fall. So, let's look at what He said and did with women *after* the fall as I believe that will shed great light on what God meant for the consequences of the fall to be or not to be for women.

I think it is critical to see what God's Word records about women and their role even after the fall because it seems many people think that the fall disqualifies women from many of the ways we see them being used in the Bible. Did you understand that? Let me say it this way. Many think that because of the fall, women are disqualified from being used by God in both ministry and leadership. I mean being a leader of both men and women in secular society and in religious leadership.

If the fall excluded women from ministry and from speaking to both men and women for God and if the fall excluded women from leadership and even leading men, would the Bible then record God using them that way? No!

If God was against it, then we shouldn't find any occasion in the Bible where God chose to use women that way.

So let me ask you a question.

Did God choose to use women after the fall in both natural and spiritual leadership and in being His minister? He did!

Even after the fall:

- God still uses women to exercise authority and dominion in the earth and over the enemy.
- God still uses women to speak for Him even to men.
- God still uses women in leadership roles, even over men, in both the secular and religious realms.

In fact, the Bible praises many women who were in leadership over men. It records women in leadership with God's blessings and at His command, with not even a hint that their gender should somehow disqualify them.

Let's look at some of them:

1. MIRIAM

I brought you up out of Egypt and redeemed you from the land of slavery. I sent Moses to lead you, also Aaron and Miriam (Micah 6:4 NIV).

Whoa! What?!

God said, "I sent Moses to lead you and Aaron to lead you and Miriam to lead you."

Wait a minute. Didn't God know Miriam was a woman? He did.

Didn't God know this was after the fall? He did.

He knew *all* of that and yet He called her and used her as a leader over the nation of Israel. Were there men in that nation that she was to lead with Moses and Aaron? There were. *God* sent her there to be a leader over all the people, leading both men and women.

Then Miriam the prophet, Aaron's sister, took a timbrel in her hand, and all the women followed her, with timbrels and dancing (Exodus 15:20 NIV).

This verse calls Miriam a prophet. A prophet or prophetess does what? They speak for God to the people. So, she wasn't just a natural leader over all of the people but she also spoke for God to all the people, leading both men and women spiritually too.

I don't think it matters that it says in this verse that it was the *women* who sang and danced with her. The Bible does *not* say she only led women; no, she was included with Moses and Aaron as leaders of the *nation*.

In fact, Miriam got in trouble because she got a little too big for her britches, if you know what I mean by that, and tried to undermine Moses, her brother, because she didn't like his choice of a wife.

Miriam and Aaron began to talk against Moses because of his Cushite wife, for he had married a Cushite. "Has the

Lord spoken only through Moses?" they asked. "Hasn't he also spoken through us?" And the Lord heard this (Numbers 12:1-2 NIV).

Why would she say that and why would Aaron agree if God had not used her to speak on His behalf to the people? She wouldn't be called a prophet or prophetess if God had not used her to speak for Him to the people, so what she said was true.

Let's read on.

(Now Moses was a very humble man, more humble than anyone else on the face of the earth.) At once the Lord said to Moses, Aaron and Miriam, "Come out to the tent of meeting, all three of you." So the three of them went out. Then the Lord came down in a pillar of cloud; he stood at the entrance to the tent and summoned Aaron and Miriam. When the two of them stepped forward, he said, "Listen to my words: When there is a prophet among you, I, the Lord, reveal myself to them in visions, I speak to them in dreams. But this is not true of my servant Moses; he is faithful in all my house. With him I speak face to face, clearly and not in riddles; he sees the form of the Lord. Why then were you not afraid to speak against my servant Moses?" (Numbers 12:3-8 NIV)

God never disputed that she was a leader. He never disputed that He used her to speak on His behalf to the people; He was just upset that she got too big for her britches, got into pride because of offense, and began to undermine Moses' leadership. God obviously really liked Moses. He had called Moses, and He *didn't* like one of His leaders undermining another.

Her competitiveness was disdainful to God. That would be like the associate pastor of our church rising up against my husband, the senior pastor, because of offense and trying to undermine his leadership to the people. Or worse yet, *me* doing that. That competitiveness is disdainful to God and nearly cost Miriam her life.

Despite the fact that Miriam was a woman and that this was after the fall, God called her to a leadership position not just over women but over men too, and God used her as a prophet to speak on His behalf to the people.

Do we see God calling and using other women in the Old Testament too? We do!

2. DEBORAH

*Then **the Lord raised up judges,** who saved them out of the hands of these raiders. Yet they would not listen to their judges but prostituted themselves to other gods and worshiped them. They quickly turned from the ways of their ancestors, who had been obedient to the Lord's commands. Whenever **the Lord raised up a judge** for them, **he was with the judge and saved them out of the hands of their enemies as long as the judge lived;** for the Lord relented because of their groaning under those who oppressed and afflicted them (Judges 2:16-18 NIV).*

These verses clearly state that the Lord was the one who raised up the judges, one of whom was Deborah.

Now Deborah, a prophet, the wife of Lappidoth, was leading Israel at that time (Judges 4:4 NIV).

Wait! Stop right there. First, Deborah is called a prophet, and a prophet or prophetess is one who speaks for God to the people. Second, this verse clearly says she was *leading* the nation of Israel at that time. She was a leader of Israel as a judge. Third, we know *God* chose her to lead the nation of Israel as Judges 2, which we looked at earlier, clearly says that *God* chose the judges.

She was both a natural and spiritual leader in that nation *over both men and women.*

Well, wait a minute, didn't God know she was a woman? He did.

Didn't God know this was after the fall? He did.

The Bible clearly states that it is God Himself who raised up the judges. Deborah was a judge raised up by God Himself, who was leading the *nation* of Israel at that time, both men and women.

Wow! Let's read on.

She held court under the Palm of Deborah between Ramah and Bethel in the hill country of Ephraim, and the Israelites went up to her to have their disputes decided. She sent for Barak son of Abinoam [a man] from Kedesh in Naphtali and said to him, "The Lord, the God of Israel, commands you: 'Go, take with you ten thousand men of Naphtali and Zebulun and lead them up to Mount Tabor'" (Judges 4:5-6 NIV).

Deborah (a woman) delivered the word of the Lord to Barak (a man). Barak wasn't just a man but he was a man who was a leader of other men. If he could gather an army of 10,000 and get them to follow him into war then he was a leader. Let's read on.

"The Lord, the God of Israel, commands you: …I will lead Sisera, the commander of Jabin's army, with his chariots and his troops to the Kishon River and give him into your hands."

Barak said to her, "If you go with me, I will go; but if you don't go with me, I won't go."

"Certainly I will go with you," said Deborah. "But because of the course you are taking, the honor will not be yours, for the Lord will deliver Sisera into the hands of a woman." So Deborah went with Barak to Kedesh. There Barak summoned Zebulun and Naphtali, and ten thousand men went up under his command. Deborah also went up with him.

Now Heber the Kenite had left the other Kenites, the descendants of Hobab, Moses' brother-in-law, and pitched his tent by the great tree in Zaanannim near Kedesh.

When they told Sisera that Barak son of Abinoam had gone up to Mount Tabor, Sisera summoned from Harosheth Haggoyim to the Kishon River all his men and his nine hundred chariots fitted with iron.

Then Deborah said to Barak, "Go! This is the day the Lord has given Sisera into your hands. Has not the Lord gone ahead of you?" *So Barak went down Mount Tabor, with ten thousand men following him (Judges 4:7-14 NIV).*

Deborah, a woman, was leading 10,001 *men* (Barak and the 10,000 men he called) by the inspiration and unction of the Holy Spirit, and they were following her, knowing she had heard from God, even though she was a woman and this was after the fall!

At Barak's advance, the Lord routed Sisera and all his chariots and army by the sword, and Sisera got down from his chariot and fled on foot.

Barak pursued the chariots and army as far as Harosheth Haggoyim, and all Sisera's troops fell by the sword; not a man was left. Sisera, meanwhile, fled on foot to the tent of Jael, the wife of Heber the Kenite, because there was an alliance between Jabin king of Hazor and the family of Heber the Kenite.

Jael went out to meet Sisera and said to him, "Come, my lord, come right in. Don't be afraid." So he entered her tent, and she covered him with a blanket.

"I'm thirsty," he said. "Please give me some water." She opened a skin of milk, gave him a drink, and covered him up.

"Stand in the doorway of the tent," he told her. "If someone comes by and asks you, 'Is anyone in there?' say 'No.'"

But Jael, Heber's wife, picked up a tent peg and a hammer and went quietly to him while he lay fast asleep, exhausted. She drove the peg through his temple into the ground, and he died.

Just then Barak came by in pursuit of Sisera, and Jael went out to meet him. "Come," she said, "I will show you the man you're looking for." So he went in with her, and there lay Sisera with the tent peg through his temple—dead.

On that day God subdued Jabin king of Canaan before the Israelites. And the hand of the Israelites pressed harder and harder against Jabin king of Canaan until they destroyed him (Judges 4:15-24 NIV).

That day, God wrought a great victory for Israel by speaking to the woman prophetess He had put in place and using *her* to lead 10,001 men to rout the army of the enemy. Then God used another woman, Jael, to kill the leader of the enemy army. God used not one, but *two* women to save the nation of Israel that day!

Could God have "raised up" a male judge? He could have, but instead He chose Deborah. Could God have spoken directly to Barak? He could have, but He chose to use Deborah to speak for Him. Could God have used one of the men to slay Sisera, the enemy commander on the battlefield? He could have, but He chose to use Jael to kill him, thus winning the battle for Israel using yet another woman. All of this God did despite the fact that they were women and this was after the fall!

The entire next chapter in this book of the Bible is a song about the great victory God won using these two women and Barak. God put this song in the Bible to celebrate the great victory He used these two women to win. Nowhere in this portion of scripture is there even a hint that somehow their gender should have disqualified them from being used by God. *God* chose to use them.

Then Deborah and Barak broke into a duet to celebrate how God had used them and Jael to win this battle.

On that day Deborah and Barak son of Abinoam sang this song:
"When the princes in Israel take the lead, when the people willingly offer themselves—praise the Lord! Hear this, you kings! Listen, you rulers! I, even I, will sing to the Lord; I will praise the Lord, the God of Israel, in song.

"When you, Lord, went out from Seir, when you marched from the land of Edom, the earth shook, the heavens poured, the clouds poured down water. The mountains quaked before the Lord, the One of Sinai, before the Lord, the God of Israel.

"In the days of Shamgar son of Anath, in the days of Jael, the highways were abandoned, travelers took to winding paths. Villagers in Israel would not fight; they held back until I, Deborah,

arose, until I arose, a mother in Israel. God chose new leaders when war came to the city gates, but not a shield or spear was seen among forty thousand in Israel. My heart is with Israel's princes, with the willing volunteers among the people. Praise the Lord!

"You who ride on white donkeys, sitting on your saddle blankets, and you who walk along the road, consider the voice of the singers at the watering places. They recite the victories of the Lord, the victories of his villagers in Israel.

"Then the people of the Lord went down to the city gates. 'Wake up, wake up, Deborah! Wake up, wake up, break out in song! Arise, Barak! Take captive your captives, son of Abinoam'" (Judges 5:1-12 NIV).

They celebrated those who heard the call and heeded the words of Deborah spoken through Barak to join the fight.

The **remnant of the nobles** *came down; the people of the Lord came down to me against the mighty. Some came from Ephraim, whose roots were in Amalek; Benjamin was with the people who followed you. From Makir* **captains came down,** *from Zebulun* **those who bear a commander's staff. The princes of Issachar were with Deborah;** *yes, Issachar was with Barak, sent under his command into the valley (Judges 5:13-15 NIV).*

Nobles came to follow her. Captains came to follow her. Those who bear a commander's staff came to follow her. Princes came to follow her. But there were those who *didn't* come.

In the districts of Reuben there was much searching of heart. Why did you stay among the sheep pens to hear the whistling for the flocks? In the districts of Reuben there was much searching of heart. Gilead stayed beyond the Jordan. And Dan, why did he linger by the ships? Asher remained on the coast and stayed in his coves. The people of Zebulun risked their very lives; so did Naphtali on the terraced fields.

Kings came, they fought, the kings of Canaan fought. At Taanach, by the waters of Megiddo, they took no plunder of silver. From the heavens the stars fought, from their courses they fought against Sisera. The river Kishon swept them away, the age-old river, the river Kishon. March on, my soul; be strong! Then thundered the horses' hooves—galloping, galloping go his mighty steeds. "Curse Meroz," said the angel of the Lord. **"Curse its people bitterly, because they did not come to help the Lord, to help the Lord against the mighty"** *(Judges 5:15-23 NIV).*

Those who refused to come and help for whatever reason, whether because she was a woman or for whatever reason, these verses say they did not come to help *the Lord*. By not helping Deborah and Barak, they were not helping the Lord. The Lord was unhappy and said they were cursed because they did not follow this woman into battle. He took it personally that they didn't follow Deborah, whom He had put in charge, and the Lord said they refused to help *Him*.

"Most blessed of women be Jael, the wife of Heber the Kenite, most blessed of tent-dwelling women. *He asked for water, and she gave him milk; in a bowl fit for nobles she brought him curdled milk. Her hand reached for the tent peg, her right hand for the workman's hammer. She struck Sisera, she crushed his head, she shattered and pierced his temple. At her feet he sank,* *he fell; there he lay. At her feet he sank, he fell; where he sank, there he fell—dead.*

"Through the window peered Sisera's mother; behind the lattice she cried out, 'Why is his chariot so long in coming? Why is the clatter of his chariots delayed?' The wisest of her ladies answer her; indeed, she keeps saying to herself, 'Are they not finding and dividing the spoils: a woman or two for each man, colorful garments as plunder for Sisera, colorful garments embroidered, highly embroidered garments for my neck—all this as plunder?'

"So may all your enemies perish, Lord! But may all who love you be like the sun when it rises in its strength." **Then the land had peace forty years** *(Judges 5:24-31 NIV).*

Their nation then had peace for 40 years because two women, after the fall, followed God. One led an army of 10,001 men into battle at the command of the Lord and led a nation to victory! The other executed the final destruction of the enemy leader. *Yay God!*

3. HULDAH

In 2 Kings 22, King Josiah has just found the Book of the Law and the king realized the anger and judgment of God was against them because they had not been keeping the law.

When the king heard the words of the Book of the Law, he tore his robes. He gave these orders to Hilkiah the priest, Ahikam son of Shaphan, Akbor son of Micaiah, Shaphan the secretary and Asaiah the king's attendant: "Go and inquire of the Lord for me and for the people and for all Judah about what is written in this book that has been found. Great is the Lord's anger that burns against us because those who have gone before us have not obeyed the words of this book; they have not acted in accordance with all that is written there concerning us."

Hilkiah the priest, Ahikam, Akbor, Shaphan and Asaiah went to speak to the **prophet Huldah, who was the wife of Shallum** *son of Tikvah, the son of Harhas, keeper of the wardrobe. She lived in Jerusalem, in the New Quarter (2 Kings 22:11-14 NIV).*

When the king realized that the anger and judgment of God was against them, he was very upset about it. So much so, he tore his robes, which was a demonstration of anguish in those days. The king instructed the priest and some of his most trusted assistants to "Go and inquire of the Lord for me." These men most certainly would have sought out the most accurate prophet in the land to inquire of God since this was an important mission from the king and the fate of their nation was on the line. Where did they go? To a woman, Huldah the prophet.

She said to them, "This is what the Lord, the God of Israel, says: Tell the man who sent you to me, 'This is what the Lord says: I am going to bring disaster on this place and its people, according to everything written in the book the king of Judah has read. Because they have forsaken me and burned incense to other gods and aroused my anger by all the idols their hands have made, my anger will burn against this place and will not be quenched.' Tell the king of Judah, who sent you to inquire of the Lord, 'This is what the Lord, the God of Israel, says concerning the words you heard: Because your heart was responsive and you humbled yourself before the Lord when you heard what I have spoken against this place and its people—that they would become a curse and be laid waste—and because you tore your robes and wept in my presence, I also have heard you, declares the Lord. Therefore I will gather you to your ancestors, and you will be buried in peace. Your eyes will not see all the disaster I am going to bring on this place.'"

So they took her answer back to the king (2 Kings 22:15-20 NIV).

Then the king called together all the elders of Judah and Jerusalem. He went up to the temple of the Lord with the people of Judah, the inhabitants of Jerusalem, the priests and the prophets—all the people from the least to the greatest. He read in their hearing all the words of the Book of the Covenant, which had been found in the temple of the Lord. The king stood by the pillar and renewed the covenant in the presence of the Lord—to follow the Lord and keep his commands, statutes and decrees with all his heart and all his soul, thus confirming the words of the covenant written in this book. Then all the people pledged themselves to the covenant (2 Kings 23:1-3 NIV).

Huldah, a woman, clearly known here as a prophet or one who speaks to the people on God's behalf, accurately brought the Word of the Lord to the male king, which the king then acted upon.

The priests, which were the spiritual leaders of the day, consulted the prophet Huldah and submitted to her spiritual leadership. All of them, priests and king alike, accepted her words as divinely spoken on behalf of God. The obedience of Judah's male leadership to God's Word spoken through a woman ignited what was probably the greatest returning to God in the history of Judah.

> *Neither before nor after Josiah was there a king like him who turned to the Lord as he did—with all his heart and with all his soul and with all his strength, in accordance with all the Law of Moses (2 Kings 23:25 NIV).*

God chose Huldah and set her as a prophet to Judah and to the king. Then God used her mightily to change an entire backslidden nation and bring it back to God, despite the fact that *she was a woman* and this was *after the fall.*

4. OTHER WOMEN USED OF GOD IN THE OLD COVENANT

There were other women who were prophets (one who spoke for God to the people) in the Old Covenant.

> *Then I made love to the **prophetess,** and she conceived and gave birth to a son. And the Lord said to me, "Name him Maher-Sha-lal-Hash-Baz" (Isaiah 8:3 NIV).*

> *There was also **a prophet, Anna, the daughter of Penuel,** of the tribe of Asher. She was very old; she had lived with her husband seven years after her marriage, and then was a widow until she was eighty-four. She never left the temple but worshiped night and day, fasting and praying. Coming up to them at that very moment, she gave thanks to God and spoke about the child to all who were looking forward to the redemption of Jerusalem (Luke 2:36-38 NIV).*

God brought deliverance to the people through the hands of other women too.

Abimelek went to the tower and attacked it. But as he approached the entrance to the tower to set it on fire, a woman dropped an upper millstone on his head and cracked his skull. Hurriedly he called to his armor-bearer, "Draw your sword and kill me, so that they can't say, 'A woman killed him.'" So his servant ran him through, and he died. When the Israelites saw that Abimelek was dead, they went home. Thus God repaid the wickedness that Abimelek had done to his father by murdering his seventy brothers (Judges 9:52-56 NIV).

Abimelek didn't want anyone to know he was killed by a woman, but God made sure it was in a couple different places of the Bible so that everyone knows.

Who killed Abimelek son of Jerub-Besheth? Didn't a woman drop an upper millstone on him from the wall, so that he died in Thebez? (2 Samuel 11:21 NIV)

What about Queen Esther who was able to save the Jewish people from annihilation?

The Bible not only acknowledges the leadership positions of Queen Esther, the Queen of Sheba, and the Queen of Chaldea but only praises and never criticizes their leadership, even over men.

Scripture does not criticize any of these women on the grounds that their having leadership and authority over men is an inappropriate role for a woman. Instead, the Old Testament presents women in spiritual and secular leadership and women speaking for God even to men as normal. Nowhere does it say these women were aberrations or special exceptions from what was normal.

God knew what He meant when He talked to Adam and Eve about the results of their sin after the fall. If some part of the fall excluded women from ministry and leadership then we should *not* see God using them that way, but He did, not just once but over and over again.

God **did not** *exclude women from leadership after the fall, and we see God Himself appointing women to both sacred and secular leadership and using them to speak for Him in ministry.*

Therefore, it is obvious that the fall does not preclude women from ministry and leadership over both men and women in both secular and spiritual leadership.

CHAPTER 5

JESUS' HEART TOWARD WOMEN

During Jesus' lifetime, one of the things He came to do was to reveal again the character and heart of the Father. By this time in history they had reduced humanity's relationship with God to a list of religious dos and don'ts that were required by a seemingly impersonal God. We know in the Old Testament that the Spirit of God only came on the priest, the prophet, and the king, but the ordinary people had no personal relationship with God.

Jesus clearly tells us that He is a reflection of the Father. When you have seen Jesus, you have seen the Father.

*Philip said, "Lord, show us the Father and that will be enough for us." Jesus answered: "Don't you know me, Philip, even after I have been among you such a long time? **Anyone who has seen me has seen the Father. How can you say, 'Show us the Father'?"** (John 14:8-9 NIV)*

***I and the Father are one** (John 10:30 NIV).*

*Do not believe me unless I do the works of my Father. But if I do them, even though you do not believe me, believe the works, that you may know and understand that **the Father is in me, and I in the Father** (John 10:37-38 NIV).*

*"I have much to say in judgment of you. But he who sent me is trustworthy, and **what I have heard from him I tell the world.**" They did not understand that he was telling them about his Father. So Jesus said, "When you have lifted up the Son of Man, then you will know that I am he and that **I do nothing on my own but speak just what the Father has taught me"** (John 8:26-28 NIV).*

*Jesus gave them this answer: "Very truly I tell you, **the Son can do nothing by himself; he can do only what he sees his Father doing, because whatever the Father does the Son also does"** (John 5:19 NIV).*

***By myself I can do nothing; I judge only as I hear, and my judgment is just, for I seek not to please myself but him who sent me** (John 5:30 NIV).*

Jesus clearly tells us that He didn't do anything on His own but He only said and did what His Father instructed Him to say and do. Because of that, when we look at Jesus' life and how He interacted with women, we can know with surety Jesus' behavior reflected not only Jesus' heart but also the heart of Father God toward women.

Let's look at Jesus and see how He interacted with women during His lifetime.

1. THE WOMAN AT THE WELL

Now he had to go through Samaria. So he came to a town in Samaria called Sychar, near the plot of ground Jacob had given to his son Joseph. Jacob's well was there, and Jesus, tired as he was from the journey, sat down by the well. It was about noon.

When a Samaritan woman came to draw water, Jesus said to her, "Will you give me a drink?" (His disciples had gone into the town to buy food.) The Samaritan woman said to him, "You are a Jew and I am a Samaritan woman. How can you ask me for a drink?" (For Jews do not associate with Samaritans.)

Jesus answered her, "If you knew the gift of God and who it is that asks you for a drink, you would have asked him and he would have given you living water."

"Sir," the woman said, "you have nothing to draw with and the well is deep. Where can you get this living water? Are you greater than our father Jacob, who gave us the well and drank from it himself, as did also his sons and his livestock?"

Jesus answered, "Everyone who drinks this water will be thirsty again, but whoever drinks the water I give them will never thirst. Indeed, the water I give them will become in them a spring of water welling up to eternal life."

The woman said to him, "Sir, give me this water so that I won't get thirsty and have to keep coming here to draw water."

He told her, "Go, call your husband and come back."

"I have no husband," she replied.

Jesus said to her, "You are right when you say you have no husband. The fact is, you have had five husbands, and the man you now have is not your husband. What you have just said is quite true."

"Sir," the woman said, "I can see that you are a prophet. Our ancestors worshiped on this mountain, but you Jews claim that the place where we must worship is in Jerusalem."

"Woman," Jesus replied, "believe me, a time is coming when you will worship the Father neither on this mountain nor in Jerusalem. You Samaritans worship what you do not know; we worship what we do know, for salvation is from the Jews. Yet a time is coming and has now come when the true worshipers will worship the Father in the Spirit and in truth, for they are the kind of worshipers the Father seeks. God is spirit, and his worshipers must worship in the Spirit and in truth" (John 4:4-24 NIV).

This is a remarkable thing Jesus was doing.

Number one: This was a woman. Men did not talk to women they did not know in that day. It was very much against their culture.

Number two: She was a Samaritan. The Jewish people of His day despised the Samaritans due to many factors, not the least of which was their ethnicity as they were only partially Jewish.

Number three: She was actively living in sin.

Each one of those things should have kept Him from talking to her. But they didn't.

Beyond those things, Jesus was showing respect for her as a person and her intellectual ability and spiritual understanding by imparting into *just **her*** these great spiritual truths about worship.

He wasn't teaching His disciples. He wasn't teaching a crowd of Jewish men. He was having a private conversation with one Samaritan woman who was living in sin. He took the time to teach her, and He knew she could grasp it. But it gets even better! Let's read on.

The woman said, "I know that Messiah" (called Christ) "is coming. When he comes, he will explain everything to us."

Then Jesus declared, "I, the one speaking to you—I am he" (John 4:25-26 NIV).

When I was reading this portion of scripture while studying on this subject, the Holy Spirit arrested me and said to me that she was the very first person to whom Jesus openly revealed His true identity, that He was the Messiah. I had to research it to make sure I had heard accurately, and it is true!

The very first person to whom Jesus entrusted Himself and revealed His true identity was to a woman. Not the disciples He was with 24/7, not to the Jews nor the Jewish leaders, but He entrusted Himself to this woman with whom society would say He never should have been speaking.

This is the longest personal conversation of Jesus' that is recorded in the Bible.

Amazing!

Just then his disciples returned and were surprised to find him talking with a woman. But no one asked, "What do you want?" or "Why are you talking with her?" (John 4:27 NIV)

When His disciples returned, they were surprised to see Him talking with a woman, let alone engaging her in deep, meaningful conversation.

Then, leaving her water jar, the woman went back to the town and said to the people, "Come, see a man who told me every-thing I ever did. Could this be the Messiah?" They came out of the town and made their way toward him (John 4:28-30 NIV).

Let's pick up with verse 39.

Many of the Samaritans from that town believed in him because of the woman's testimony, "He told me everything I ever did." So when the Samaritans came to him, they urged him to stay with

*them, and he stayed two days. And because of his words many
more became believers.*

*They said to the woman, "We no longer believe just because
of what you said; now we have heard for ourselves, and we know
that this man really is the Savior of the world" (John 4:39-42
NIV).*

This woman ended up being a very effective evangelist and
brought many to belief in Christ as the Messiah, and beyond all
of that, I love the respect and dignity Jesus showed to her despite
it being totally against the culture of His day.

2. THE WOMAN CAUGHT IN ADULTERY

Jesus resisted the pressure put on Him by the teachers of the
law and the Pharisees who wanted to stone the woman caught
in adultery and instead Jesus decided to show her mercy. Really
by the letter of the law she should have been stoned, but they
knew Jesus would want to show her mercy. So they brought
her to Jesus hoping to trap Him so they could accuse Him of
not following the Law if He didn't side with them and stone
her.

*The teachers of the law and the Pharisees brought in a woman
caught in adultery. They made her stand before the group (John
8:3 NIV).*

For someone to be caught in the very act of adultery, there
had to be more than one person involved. Where was the man?
Him they let go, but they dragged *her* out into the street to be
publicly judged. Hmmm, how interesting!

And said to Jesus, "Teacher, this woman was caught in the act of adultery. In the Law Moses commanded us to stone such women. Now what do you say?" They were using this question as a trap, in order to have a basis for accusing him.

But Jesus bent down and started to write on the ground with his finger. When they kept on questioning him, he straightened up and said to them, "Let any one of you who is without sin be the first to throw a stone at her." Again he stooped down and wrote on the ground.

At this, those who heard began to go away one at a time, the older ones first, until only Jesus was left, with the woman still standing there. Jesus straightened up and asked her, "Woman, where are they? Has no one condemned you?"

"No one, sir," she said.

"Then neither do I condemn you," Jesus declared. "Go now and leave your life of sin" (John 8:4-11 NIV).

Jesus was really the only one there who could have been "the first to throw a stone at her" because He was the only one present who truly was without sin. As Jesus' words convicted the hearts of her accusers about their own sin, one by one they left. With no accusers remaining, Jesus was the only one there who could have condemned her, but He chose to show her mercy instead, which was totally against the culture of the day.

3. MARY, THE SISTER OF MARTHA

Jesus the rabbi, or teacher, validated Mary's desire to learn and to be taught over serving the men.

In a time when women were not allowed to be educated, Jesus validated Mary's decision to sit at His feet and be taught about ministry and the Kingdom over her "womanly duties." This was extremely radical for His day.

As Jesus and his disciples were on their way, he came to a village where a woman named Martha opened her home to him. She had a sister called Mary, who sat at the Lord's feet listening to what he said.

But Martha was distracted by all the preparations that had to be made. She came to him and asked, "Lord, don't you care that my sister has left me to do the work by myself? Tell her to help me!"

"Martha, Martha," the Lord answered, "you are worried and upset about many things, but few things are needed—or indeed only one. Mary has chosen what is better, and it will not be taken away from her" (Luke 10:38-42 NIV).

When we see Mary sitting at the feet of Jesus, we don't really understand the cultural implications of what she was doing. We imagine her sitting at Jesus' feet, looking up at Him adoringly while He taught; but to "sit at a teacher's feet" was the position of a disciple, one who was being trained to be like the teacher.

Paul used that same terminology to describe his own religious training.

*I am a Jew, born in Tarsus of Cilicia but reared in this city. **At the feet of Gamaliel** I was educated according to the strictest care in the Law of our fathers, being ardent [even a zealot] for God, as all of you are today (Acts 22:3 AMPC).*

Notice the verbiage Paul used here. He said he sat at the feet of Gamaliel, and by that he means Gamaliel educated and trained him for service to God. When we read this, we don't think of Paul sitting at the feet of Gamaliel and looking up at him all goo-goo eyed. No, that is normal first-century phraseology for someone being discipled and trained up by someone else in the ministry.

In other words, Mary took the position, in this room full of men, as a disciple, one being trained up in the ministry. Her putting herself in that room at Jesus' feet was *so* against the culture of the day, but Jesus validated her choice to be there and to learn.

So, if Jesus validated Mary's choice to sit at His feet and be trained as a disciple and Jesus was not opposed to women disciples, then why were the original 12 disciples all men? We know that all of us as followers of Christ, both men and women, are now disciples of Christ, but why didn't Jesus choose any women to be listed among His initial 12 disciples?

I think there are several reasons for this.

1. I think that since they traveled everywhere together, camping out and staying together in people's homes, it made sense for all to be male to avoid scandal or even the appearance of evil.
2. The appointment of 12 Jewish men paralleled the 12 sons of Israel and reenforced the symbolism of the church as the "new Israel."

I do not believe the exclusion of women from being among the original 12 disciples excludes women from leadership or discipleship in any form. There were no Gentiles among those 12 disciples either, but we obviously have Gentile disciples and leaders today.

In fact, Jesus had many women disciples who followed His ministry.

*After this, Jesus traveled about from one town and village to another, proclaiming the good news of the Kingdom of God. The Twelve were with him, and **also some women** who had been cured of evil spirits and diseases: **Mary** (called Magdalene) from whom seven demons had come out; **Joanna** the wife of Chuza, the manager of Herod's household; **Susanna;** and **many others**. These women were helping to support them out of their own means (Luke 8:1-3 NIV).*

Jesus had many women disciples and followers.

So, we saw earlier in Luke 10, Jesus validated Mary's choice to sit at His feet and be trained as a disciple. Later, we see this same Mary, the sister of Martha, in yet another profound moment with Jesus.

Six days before the Passover, Jesus came to Bethany, where Lazarus lived, whom Jesus had raised from the dead. Here a dinner was given in Jesus' honor. Martha served, while Lazarus was among those reclining at the table with him. Then Mary took about a pint of pure nard, an expensive perfume; she poured it on Jesus' feet and wiped his feet with her hair. And the house was filled with the fragrance of the perfume.

But one of his disciples, Judas Iscariot, who was later to betray him, objected, "Why wasn't this perfume sold and the money given to the poor? It was worth a year's wages." He did not say this because he cared about the poor but because he was a thief; as keeper of the money bag, he used to help himself to what was put into it.

"Leave her alone," Jesus replied. "It was intended that she should save this perfume for the day of my burial. You will always have the poor among you, but you will not always have me" (John 12:1-8 NIV).

Jesus defended and protected Mary, but He also said something very interesting. He said, "It was intended that she should save this perfume for the day of my burial."

Let's look at it in the Amplified Classic.

But Jesus said, Let her alone. It was [intended] that she should keep it for the time of My preparation for burial. [She has kept it that she might have it for the time of My embalming] (John 12:7 AMPC).

Let's look at it in the Young's Literal Translation.

Jesus, therefore, said, "Suffer her; for the day of my embalming she hath kept it" (John 12:7 YLT).

Mary understood what even many of Jesus' closest followers and disciples did *not* understand—He was not only going to have to give His life, but the time had come for Him to do so. The Bible said she had kept that perfume back in reserve for the time of His embalming, and she brought it out *now* when He was days away from being crucified. Equally important, Jesus knew that Mary knew His time had come. I am certain that meant so much to Him. She understood and she was in that moment with Him when so many around Him were totally oblivious to the depth of what He was facing and the weight of it for Him as the time of His crucifixion approached. This was a profound and tender moment between Jesus and Mary that most certainly brought Jesus comfort.

4. MARY MAGDALENE

After His death, burial, and resurrection, Jesus chose a woman to be the first one to whom He showed Himself alive, and He made her a preacher of the Good News.

> He asked her, "Woman, why are you crying? Who is it you are looking for?"
>
> Thinking he was the gardener, she said, "Sir, if you have carried him away, tell me where you have put him, and I will get him."
>
> Jesus said to her, "Mary."
>
> She turned toward him and cried out in Aramaic, "Rabboni!" (which means "Teacher").
>
> Jesus said, "Do not hold on to me, for I have not yet ascended to the Father. Go instead to my brothers and tell them, 'I am ascending to my Father and your Father, to my God and your God.'"
>
> Mary Magdalene went to the disciples with the news: "I have seen the Lord!" And she told them that he had said these things to her (John 20:15-18 NIV).
>
> Mary Magdalene found the disciples and told them, "I have seen the Lord!" Then she gave them his message (John 20:18 NLT).

Within hours of His resurrection, Jesus used Mary to be the first preacher of His resurrection. Really, an apostle is a sent one, and I don't think it would do harm to the scripture to say she was the first apostle to the apostles.

This is the essence of preaching. God tells you what to say and to whom, and you just deliver His message.

If Jesus had wanted to, He could have simply told Mary, "Go get My disciples, I want to tell them something." But He didn't.

He told *her* to deliver a message for Him, and He told her what to say and to whom to say it. Ladies and gentlemen, that *is* ministry! You just deliver His messages to whomever He tells you to deliver them.

You go to God and He tells you what to speak to whom.

It was no mistake that God gave Mary, a woman, the honor of being the first person to bear witness of His resurrection and to deliver the message to His male disciples, telling them about His resurrection.

All throughout His life, Jesus showed the value of women even though His doing so was very much against the culture of the day. He respected the women He encountered and taught and trained them when the opportunities to do so arose, even though others around Him didn't understand or like it. He trusted them to deliver His messages. He even revealed great truths first to some of these women, such as His identity as the Messiah and His resurrection. He resisted the pressure brought to bear on Him by the religious people to be merciless and harsh to them.

In doing all of this, we see not only was Jesus' heart toward women, but we understand that because Jesus did and said only what He was inspired by the Father to do and say, His life and ministry was an accurate reflection of the tender heart of Father God toward women as well.

CHAPTER 6

PROPHECIES REGARDING LAST-DAYS WOMEN

But in fact the ministry Jesus has received is as superior to theirs as the covenant of which he is mediator is superior to the old one, since the new covenant is established on better promises (Hebrews 8:6 NIV).

We know that the New Covenant is superior to the Old Covenant and is based on new and better promises—except when it comes to women, right?

We have clearly seen how God, knowing what He meant when He told Adam and Eve about the consequences of the fall, chose women in the Old Covenant to be ministers and to speak for Him, even to the men. He chose them to be both secular and spiritual leaders over both men and women and *He* Himself set them in place. If something about the fall disqualified women from ministry and leadership, then God would have known it and He would not have used them as He did after the fall.

So, would the New Testament promises be better in every way except when it comes to women? *No!* Would a woman be less usable by God just because Christ died and redeemed us to Himself? *No!*

Old Testament prophets prepare us for women taking even greater prophetic and ministerial roles in the New Covenant:

*And afterward, I will pour out my Spirit on all people. Your sons **and daughters** will prophesy, your old men will dream dreams, your young men will see visions. Even on my servants, **both men and women**, I will pour out my Spirit in those days (Joel 2:28-29 NIV).*

This scripture's fulfillment began on the day or Pentecost.

When the day of Pentecost came, they were all together in one place. Suddenly a sound like the blowing of a violent wind came from heaven and filled the whole house where they were sitting. They saw what seemed to be tongues of fire that separated and came to rest on each of them. All of them were filled with the Holy Spirit and began to speak in other tongues as the Spirit enabled them.

Now there were staying in Jerusalem God-fearing Jews from every nation under heaven. When they heard this sound, a crowd came together in bewilderment, because each one heard their own language being spoken. Utterly amazed, they asked: "Aren't all these who are speaking Galileans? Then how is it that each of us hears them in our native language? Parthians, Medes and Elamites; residents of Mesopotamia, Judea and Cappadocia, Pontus and Asia, Phrygia and Pamphylia, Egypt and the parts of Libya near Cyrene; visitors from Rome (both Jews and converts to Judaism); Cretans and Arabs—we hear them declaring the wonders of God in our own tongues!" Amazed and perplexed, they asked one another, "What does this mean?"

Some, however, made fun of them and said, "They have had too much wine."

*Then Peter stood up with the Eleven, raised his voice and addressed the crowd: "Fellow Jews and all of you who live in Jerusalem, let me explain this to you; listen carefully to what I say. These people are not drunk, as you suppose. It's only nine in the morning! No, **this is what was spoken by the prophet Joel:***

*"'**In the last days, God says, I will pour out my Spirit on all people. Your sons and daughters will prophesy**, your young men will see visions, your old men will dream dreams. **Even on my servants, both men and women, I will pour out my Spirit in those days, and they will prophesy.** I will show wonders in the heavens above and signs on the earth below, blood and fire and billows of smoke. The sun will be turned to darkness and the moon to blood before the coming of the great and glorious day of the Lord. And everyone who calls on the name of the Lord will be saved'" (Acts 2:1-21 NIV).*

According to Peter, the day of Pentecost was the beginning of the Last Days and the beginning of what was spoken through the prophet Joel. Joel prophesied that in the Last Days, God would pour out His Spirit on *all people* and that your sons *and daughters* will prophesy. And that on men and women alike He is pouring out His Spirit and they *will* prophesy!

CHAPTER 7

PAUL AND WOMEN

I want to look into the New Testament teaching on women and specifically at Paul's teaching on this subject. But before we do, I think we need to establish whether Paul was opposed to women in ministry. That is important because it affects how we interpret Paul's words on that matter.

When you correctly understand Paul, you will see that he was a champion of women using their gifts in a corporate church setting. I am going to give you some background here to help you understand Paul and the time in which he lived.

Though I might also have confidence in the flesh. If any other man thinketh that he hath whereof he might trust in the flesh, I more: circumcised the eighth day, of the stock of Israel, of the tribe of Benjamin, an Hebrew of the Hebrews; as touching the law, a Pharisee; concerning zeal, persecuting the church; touching the righteousness which is in the law, blameless (Philippians 3:4-6 KJV).

This was the apostle Paul talking about his background. He was not a casual Jew. He was radically Jewish, zealous to be a good Jew and to defend his Jewish faith at all costs.

In the sect of Judaism of which Paul was a member, women were not valued at all. In fact, every morning Paul would recite his prayers and that meant, among other things, Paul would pray, "God, I thank You that I was born a man, not a woman."

How might that affect the thinking of a young man if he said that every morning?

In the Jewish culture of Paul's day, women and men did not mix socially. No self-respecting Jewish leader would even be seen talking to a woman in public. That is why the disciples were so shocked to find Jesus engaged in a deep, meaningful conversation with the woman at the well. It just wasn't done in that day.

Now in addition to the Jewish culture in which Paul was raised, they were being occupied at that time by Rome. The culture of these first-century Romans was also not affirming to women, and in this day Roman women just stayed at home. They had no legal status, and in fact, girls were considered the property of their father until they married. When they married, they became the legal property of their husbands. Most were not taught to read or write, and they were not even considered citizens of Rome. They were not allowed in public meetings and rarely were women seen in public. They were expected to just stay at home.

Now because of the fall and Adam and Eve's sin and the enmity between the woman and Satan (Genesis 3:14-15), it seems that with every generation, the status of women kept being reduced until this was the state of things at the time of Paul.

Paul was steeped in his sect of Judaism and in the Roman culture of that day, which was forced upon them by their occupiers, both of which thought poorly of women.

That was the thinking of the day, and it would have been Paul's thinking too until something glorious, something amazing happened!

Paul met Jesus!

We know Paul got born again after Jesus appeared to him on the road to Damascus. But beyond that, *Paul said Jesus Himself taught him the principles of the New Covenant!*

But I certify you, brethren, that the gospel which was preached of me is not after man. For I neither received it of man, neither was I taught it, but by the revelation of Jesus Christ (Galatians 1:11-12 KJV).

Paul came out of those times when Jesus Himself taught him with great revelation about a number of different things, including the revelation that we see here in Galatians 3.

For ye are all the children of God by faith in Christ Jesus. For as many of you as have been baptized into Christ have put on Christ. There is neither Jew nor Greek, there is neither bond nor free, there is neither male nor female: for ye are all one in Christ Jesus (Galatians 3:26-28 KJV).

In saying there is neither Jew nor Greek, the racial division was eliminated in Christ. He said there is neither bond nor free in the Body of Christ (the church), so there should be no class distinction. He then said there is neither male nor female, so there is no gender division, because we are all now one in Christ Jesus.

This revelation *from Jesus Himself* was totally against Paul's Jewish culture and totally against the Roman culture of the day. This statement here in Galatians 3 was a radical, radical statement that totally opposed everything Paul had believed to that point and all he had been taught all of his life.

To Paul's credit, when he heard the truth, he was able to let go of his upbringing and his religious traditions and embrace the truth he was taught by Jesus.

Jesus taught him that now in Christ there was no distinction between male and female, meaning one was not greater than the other, thus setting things back to the way God intended in the garden before the fall when man and woman stood face to face, hand in hand, ruling and reigning together. When he got this truth, Paul did something incredibly radical! He threw open the doors of the church meetings and women were invited to church! It was unthinkable for his day!

Many women had never attended a public assembly before this. They were kept at home, out of sight. Therefore, when the women started coming in, they had no experience in public meetings. They weren't ignorant; they had just never done it before, so they didn't know how to behave while they were there at the church meetings with all the guys.

Then Paul goes on even further.

But every woman that prayeth or prophesieth with her head uncovered dishonoureth her head: for that is even all one as if she were shaven (1 Corinthians 11:5 KJV).

We will get to the head coverings in a minute but there is something here I want you to see.

Not only did Paul allow women to come to church, but he allowed women to pray publicly and openly and prophesy publicly and openly in the meetings.

Prophecy is speaking to the people for God under the inspiration of the Holy Spirit. Simple prophecy is speaking by the inspiration of the Holy Spirit to bring edification, exhortation, and comfort.

Isn't that what most sermons are? Speaking by the inspiration of God the Holy Spirit for edification, exhortation, and comfort. Let's look at it in the Amplified Classic.

And any woman who [publicly] prays or prophesies (teaches, refutes, reproves, admonishes, or comforts) when she is bare-headed dishonors her head (her husband); it is the same as [if her head were] shaved (1 Corinthians 11:5 AMPC).

Any woman who publicly prays or prophesies (teaches, refutes, reproves, admonishes, or comforts)—the Amplified Classic is even more explicit than the King James Version, saying women can pray, prophesy, teach, refute, reprove, admonish, or comfort, and they are able to do it publicly, in the service.

Paul allowed women to use their gifts *publicly*, including the vocal gifts! He just wanted it done in a certain way (with a head covering) when they used their gifts in the public church meeting.

Was Paul making the admonition to wear head coverings a requirement for every woman who would speak from the early church even to our day? I don't think so, and let me explain why.

We know from historical records that in the first century the custom was that most women kept their head covered by a shawl or cloth for modesty and that the only women who let their hair down and did not wear head coverings were, how shall I say this, women with loose morals and women of ill repute. Some prostitutes even had their head completely shaved. I think Paul was particularly sensitive to this when it came to the church at Corinth because the most prominent secular religion in this area was the worship of Bacchus. In short, Bacchus was the party god and his "worship" basically consisted of drunken orgies.

Because of this, you can easily see how Paul would not want these women who are now speaking and ministering in the new Christian church to look like they were loose in their morals or looking like the women in Bacchus' temple.

In verse 16, Paul clearly referred to head coverings as their "custom" in that day, thus I do believe it was just their custom and not a requirement for all women ministers and believers. This is the only place in the New Testament that says women should wear them while ministering in the public service.

If it were an ongoing requirement, I think it would be spelled out clearly everywhere in the New Testament, since 50 percent or more of Christians are women and thus it would be a requirement that would affect a *lot* of believers.

Plus, the Bible itself says in the mouth of two or three witnesses let every matter be confirmed and this is the one and only place it is taught.

This is the third time I am coming to you. In the mouth of two or three witnesses shall every word be established (2 Corinthians 13:1 KJV).

But if he will not hear thee, then take with thee one or two more, that in the mouth of two or three witnesses every word may be established (Matthew 18:16 KJV).

(See Appendix B for more details on 1 Corinthians 11.)

Was Paul against women ministering in the church? Not according to these verses, but let's keep looking at what the scriptures Paul wrote can show us about his opinion of women ministering and even serving in leadership positions in the church.

I commend unto you Phebe our sister, which is a servant of the church which is at Cenchrea: that ye receive her in the Lord, as becometh saints, and that ye assist her in whatsoever business she hath need of you: for she hath been a succourer of many, and of myself also (Romans 16:1-2 KJV).

In verse 1, the English King James Version Bible calls Phebe a servant. But really the word Paul used is the Greek word *diakonos*. According to *Strong's Exhaustive Concordance of the Bible,* that word means "an attendant, i.e. (genitive case) a waiter (at table or in other menial duties); specially, a Christian teacher and pastor (technically, a deacon or deaconess)."

Paul used this word 21 times in the epistles he wrote. Seventeen out of 21 times the King James translators translated that word as "a minister." Paul used this word to even describe the work done by Paul himself, Apollos, Timothy, and the apostles.

Seventeen out of 21 times, the King James translators translated that word as "a minister." Three times the translators translated that word as "deacon." Only once was that word translated "servant" and it is here in this verse regarding Phebe. Hmmm.

The Young's Literal Translation calls her a minister.

And I commend you to Phebe our sister—being a ministrant of the assembly that [is] in Cenchrea (Romans 16:1 YLT).

But the literal translation doesn't just say she was a minister, it says she was a leader with Paul too.

And I commend you to Phebe our sister—being a ministrant of the assembly that [is] in Cenchrea—that ye may receive her in the Lord, as doth become saints, and may assist her in whatever matter she may have need of you—for she also became a leader of many, and of myself (Romans 16:1-2 YLT).

In the literal translation, Paul said she was a minister and that she was a *leader* of many. Some have made the argument that Paul says she was a leader even of himself, though I do not see corroborating evidence that she was a leader over Paul in other parts of the scriptures.

The King James Version calls her a succorer. That is a word we do not use often.

According to *Strong's Exhaustive Concordance*, the Greek word Paul used here translated "succorer" is *prostatis*: "feminine of a derivative of word 4291; a patroness, i.e. assistant."

That word is a feminine version of 4291, which is the Greek word *proistemi*: "to stand before, i.e. (in rank) to preside, or (by implication) to practice: King James Version: maintain, be over, rule."

I think it is fascinating that her leadership is all over these verses in the original language but in the English translations it is watered down to *servant* or *helper*.

Paul publicly honored this woman minister. She obviously was someone Paul highly respected and honored for the work she was doing and for her leadership. He specifically tells them to go out of their way for her and do everything they can to help her because of the work she was doing. I don't see him doing that for anyone else, not even for the other male ministers he mentions.

If Paul was opposed to women being ministers and deacons, he wouldn't have publicly recognized her as one and publicly honored her for her work as a minister or deacon. And he certainly would not have asked them to go out of their way to help her for her works' sake.

I commend unto you Phebe our sister, which is a servant of the church which is at Cenchrea: that ye receive her in the Lord, as becometh saints, and that ye assist her in whatsoever business she hath need of you: for she hath been a succourer of many, and of myself also. Greet Priscilla and Aquila my helpers in Christ Jesus: who have for my life laid down their own necks: unto whom not only I give thanks, but also all the churches of the Gentiles (Romans 16:1-4 KJV).

I want you to notice that Paul called out *both* Priscilla and Aquila. The King James Version says they are his "helpers." The actual Greek word he used is *sunergos,* which means a co-laborer, i.e. coadjutor.

The literal translation of verse 3 is this:

Salute Priscilla and Aquilas, my fellow-workmen in Christ Jesus (Romans 16:3 YLT).

Paul calls them both his fellow workmen in Christ Jesus.

Almost every time Paul mentions Priscilla and Aquila he calls her name first, which was against the culture of the day. Some Greek scholars believe that her name coming first could indicate she had the greater ministry gift and was most certainly the more prominent of the two.

Priscilla was known throughout early church history as being a *powerful* teacher of the Word. So much so, some church leaders in the second and third century thought Priscilla may have been the writer of the book of Hebrews, although we do not know for sure who wrote it. My point is that Priscilla was known for being a *powerful* pastor, minister, and teacher of the Word. Paul often mentions both Priscilla and Aquila and says they were co-laborers in the work of the ministry with him.

We can see Priscilla working in the ministry in the book of Acts.

And a certain Jew named Apollos, born at Alexandria, an elo-quent man, and mighty in the scriptures, came to Ephesus. This man was instructed in the way of the Lord; and being fervent in the spirit, he spake and taught diligently the things of the Lord, knowing only the baptism of John. And he began to speak boldly in the synagogue: whom when Aquila and Priscilla had heard, they took him unto them, and expounded unto him the way of God more perfectly (Acts 18:24-26 KJV).

Both Priscilla and Aquila pulled Apollos, a man, aside and taught him the way of God more accurately. Nowhere in the scriptures does it say that anyone objected or that Priscilla shouldn't have been teaching Apollos because he is a man and she is a woman.

Let's read on in Romans 16.

Likewise greet the church that is in their house. Salute my well-beloved Epaenetus, who is the firstfruits of Achaia unto Christ. Greet Mary, who bestowed much labour on us. Salute Andronicus and Junia, my kinsmen, and my fellow-prisoners, who are of note among the apostles, who also were in Christ before me (Romans 16:5-7 KJV).

Junia here is a woman and Paul called her an apostle.

Not only did Paul call her an apostle but he said Andronicus and she were "of note" among the apostles, which means they were remarkable or eminent among the apostles. The Greek word used there, which is translated "of note," is *episemose,* which means remarkable, i.e. (figuratively) eminent.

Paul acknowledged a woman apostle and not only that but said she was a remarkable or eminent apostle.

The word *eminent* means "someone in a position of prominence or superiority; a person of high rank or attainments."

Let's read on in Romans 16.

Greet Amplias my beloved in the Lord. Salute Urbane, our helper in Christ, and Stachys my beloved. Salute Apelles approved in Christ. Salute them which are of Aristobulus' household. Salute Herodion my kinsman. Greet them that be of the household of Narcissus, which are in the Lord. Salute Tryphena and Tryphosa, who labour in the Lord. Salute the beloved Persis, which laboured much in the Lord (Romans 16:8-12 KJV).

Let's stop here. Tryphena and Tryphosa were twin sisters who were believed to have had some pastoral responsibilities in the first century, and Paul said they labored in the Lord.

Also in that verse is the name Persis, which is a female name, and Paul says she labored much in the Lord.

Salute Tryphena and Tryphosa, who labour in the Lord. Salute the beloved Persis, which laboured much in the Lord. Salute

Rufus chosen in the Lord, and his mother and mine. Salute Asyncritus, Phlegon, Hermas, Patrobas, Hermes, and the brethren which are with them. Salute Philologus, and Julia, Nereus, and his sister, and Olympas, and all the saints which are with them (Romans 16:12-15 KJV).

In this list of notable pastors in the early church are Julia and Olympas, both female, as well as Nereus' sister, whose name we do not know.

I want you to notice how many women ministers Paul acknowledged in this passage without objection from Paul about their ministry and with no indication that their gender should in some way disqualify them from ministry or even being pastors or apostles.

Where else did Paul acknowledge women ministers?

Now I appeal to Euodia and Syntyche. Please, because you belong to the Lord, settle your disagreement. And I ask you, my true partner, to help these two women, for they worked hard with me in telling others the Good News. They worked along with Clement and the rest of my co-workers, whose names are written in the Book of Life (Philippians 4:2-3 NLT).

Euodia and Syntyche were evangelists who worked with Paul. He lauds them for their hard work with him in telling others the Good News. Paul's ministry teams were loaded with women whom he lauded for their hard work in the ministry.

Where else in the New Testament do we see women in ministry or leadership in the church? Luke noted that Philip had daughters who ministered.

Leaving the next day, we reached Caesarea and stayed at the house of Philip the evangelist, one of the Seven. He had four unmarried daughters who prophesied (Acts 21:8-9 NIV).

Second John was written to what is called in the King James Version the "elect lady."

The elder unto the elect lady and her children, whom I love in the truth; and not I only, but also all they that have known the truth (2 John 1:1 KJV).

The word translated "lady" here is *kyria,* which is the female form of the word *kuriotes,* which means "mastery, ruler, government, or dominion, supreme in authority."

Her being called the "elect" or in some versions "chosen," *kyria,* indicates that she was specifically chosen to lead this congregation.

There are also a number of women Paul and other New Testament writers mentioned who had churches in their house, such as Chloe, Nympha, Apphia, Lydia, and more. *Most* churches were in people's homes in the early days of Christianity since they didn't have church buildings yet. Most of the time those women are regarded as pastors of those house churches, but since the Bible doesn't specifically say they were pastors I didn't include them here as definitively pastors, but they well could have been.

I want you to notice in Romans 16 that Paul did not say, "Phebe is coming to you. Poor deluded woman thinks she is a minister or a deacon." No! *Paul* called her a minister or a deacon. *Paul* called Junia an apostle. *Paul* called out and acknowledged the work of a number of women ministers.

Was Paul opposed to women in the ministry? *He was not!*

Throughout the New Testament, women were acknowledged by Paul and other New Testament writers as being used by God in the ministry. Not only were women regarded as ministers, they were *leaders* in the body of Christ, and their leadership roles were acknowledged without even a hint that they should not have been in those leadership roles because they were women.

CHAPTER 8

WHO MAY MINISTER?

Now we know that the Word of God when rightly divided does not contradict itself, so we are going to jump into the New Testament and see if we can figure out what some of those hard verses on women and women in ministry actually mean when rightly divided.

Let's start by looking at the qualifications for New Testament ministry and leadership in ministry.

This is a true saying, if a man desire the office of a bishop, he desireth a good work. A bishop then must be blameless, the husband of one wife, vigilant, sober, of good behaviour, given to hospitality, apt to teach; not given to wine, no striker, not greedy of filthy lucre; but patient, not a brawler, not covetous; one that ruleth well his own house, having his children in subjection with all gravity; (for if a man know not how to rule his own house, how shall he take care of the church of God?) Not a novice, lest being lifted up with pride he fall into the condemnation of the devil. Moreover he must have a good report of them which are without; lest he fall into reproach and the snare of the devil. Likewise must the deacons be grave, not doubletongued, not given to much wine, not greedy of filthy lucre; holding the mystery of the faith in a pure conscience. And let these also first be proved; then let them use the office of a deacon, being found blameless. Even so must their wives be grave, not slanderers, sober, faithful in all things. Let the deacons be the husbands of one wife, ruling their children and their own houses well. For they that have used the office of a deacon well purchase to themselves a good degree, and great boldness in the faith which is in Christ Jesus (1 Timothy 3:1-13 KJV).

Verses 1-7 give the qualifications of a bishop. What office are we talking about when we are talking about a bishop?

According to my Merriam Webster's dictionary app on my phone the definition of *bishop* is as follows:

1: someone having spiritual or ecclesiastical supervision over others: such as

a: an Anglican, Eastern Orthodox, or Roman Catholic clergyperson ranking above a priest, having authority to ordain and confirm, and typically governing a diocese

b: any of various Protestant clerical officials who superintend other clergy

I guess the closest thing in our vocabulary and understanding would be someone who pastors and oversees other pastors. For sure we are talking about a high leadership position.

When I was seeking the Lord for clarity on this because these verses are *so masculine* in the King James Version of the Bible, the Lord directed me to look it up in the interlinear and look at the original words that Paul used, and so I did.

Their Greek sentences are laid out differently than in our modern English language, so the sentence structure is weird to us, but I want you to see exactly what Paul said.

3:1	πιστός	ὁ		λόγος.	Εἴ τις		ἐπισκοπῆς	ὀρέγεται,	καλοῦ
	true	This	is	a saying,	If a man	the	office of a bishop,	desire	good
	4103	3588	9999	3056	1536	9999	1984	3713	2570
	Pistós	ho		lógos	Eí-tis		episkopeés	orégetai	kaloú

ἔργου	ἐπιθυμεῖ.
a work.	he desireth
2041	1937
érgou	epithumeí

Remember, in the interlinear all words are assigned a number based on the Strong's Exhaustive Concordance so that the Greek words can easily be looked up for meaning. When the translators added a word for clarity it was assigned the number 9999, which indicates those words aren't in the original Greek text. They were just added by the those who translated the Bible into English "for clarity."

In looking at the interlinear for 1 Timothy 3:1, the phrase "If a man" is the Greek word *eitis*. That is Strong's NT word 1536—*ei tis* (i tis), from NT:1487 and NT:5100, which means "if any."

The words Paul used here are *not* masculine but are gender inclusive!

In the original language it says "If any the office of a bishop desire."

Then I noticed the words "he desireth," which is also masculine in the English King James Version. So, let's look up the actual Greek words that were spoken and see if it says *he* or refers just to males in any way.

The words "he desireth" is word NT:1937 *epithumeo*, from NT:1909 and NT:2372: "to set the heart upon, i.e. long for (rightfully or otherwise)."

That masculine word "he" in front of "desireth" is not in the original text or in the meaning of the word "desireth." It was added by the King James Version translators.

Nowhere in the qualifications for church leadership, here in 1 Timothy or in Titus 1, are there any masculine pronouns or anything that would make these qualifications for ministry for males only! Contrary to a lot of translations, *everything* Paul listed in the requirements for church leadership is gender-neutral. There are *no masculine* pronouns used here or in Titus. While some translations like the King James Version made it all masculine when it was not, some got it right.

Here is a trustworthy saying: Whoever aspires to be an overseer desires a noble task (1 Timothy 3:1 NIV).

In many of these translations, the word *he* is sometimes added, even though it is not in the original language. In the original language, there are no masculine pronouns used anywhere in the passages of 1 Timothy and Titus in which the qualifications for ministerial leadership are laid out. There is no indication that these verses require one to be male to qualify for the ministry or leadership in the ministry.

When the Lord first brought me here and showed me that the actual words Paul spoke are gender-neutral, my mind was blown! I grew up in full gospel churches that prided themselves on being true to the scriptures, but I had never heard that taught, not once in my over 50 years of listening to sermons.

So then I said, "Okay, Lord, but what about verse 2? It says, 'the husband of one wife,' that is masculine." He said, "Look at it!"

² δεῖ	οὖν	τὸν	ἐπίσκοπον	ἀνεπίλημπτον	εἶναι,	μιᾶς	γυναικὸς		ἄνδρα,
must	then	A	bishop	blameless,	be	of one	wife,	the	husband
1163	3767	3588	1985	423	1511	3391	1135	9999	435
Deí	oún	tón	epískopon	anepíleempton	eínai	miás	gunaikós		ándra

νηφάλιον	σώφρονα	κόσμιον	φιλόξενον	διδακτικόν,
vigilant,	sober,	of good behaviour,	given to hospitality,	apt to teach;
3524	4998	2887	5382	1317
neefálion	soófrona	kósmion	filóxenon	didaktikón

Are you ready for this? Let's read back over that slowly: "must then a bishop blameless, be of one wife, the husband." *Hold up!* In the interlinear the word *the* has 9999 under it, which means what? That word is not in the original text. The translators added it "for clarity."

So, let's take out the word the translators added and read it like Paul wrote it.

"Must then a bishop blameless, be of one wife, husband vigilant, sober, of good behaviour, given to hospitality, apt to teach."

"Be of one wife, husband." That would indicate to me that it could go either way and be of one wife or one husband depending on the sex of the bishop. A male bishop should have only one wife, a female bishop should have only one husband.

3	μὴ	πάροινον	μὴ		πλήκτην,	ἀλλὰ	ἐπιεικῆ
	Not no	given to wine,	not	greedy of filthy lucre;	striker,	but	patient,
	3361	3943	3361	<9999>	4131	235	1933
	meé	pároinon	meé		pleékteen	allá	epieikeé

ἄμαχον	ἀφιλάργυρον,
not a brawler,	not covetous;
269	866
ámachon	afilárguron

4	τοῦ	ἰδίου	οἴκου	καλῶς	προϊστάμενον,		τέκνα	ἔχοντα	ἐν	ὑποταγῇ,
		his own	house,	well	One that ruleth	his	children	having	in	subjection
	3588	2398	3624	2573	4291	9999	5043	2192	1722	5292
	toú	idíou	oíkou	kaloós	proistámenon		tékna	échonta	en	hupotageé

μετὰ	πάσης	σεμνότητος
with	all	gravity;
3326	3956	4587
metá	pásees	semnóteetos

There are seemingly two masculine pronouns here: "his own house" and "his children." But let's look at it.

In fact, the word translated "his own" is specifically gender-neutral.

It is word NT:2398, *idios:* "of uncertain affinity, pertaining to self, i.e. *one's own;* by implication, private or separate."

When it comes to the words "his children," the word *his* is a 9999 word, which means it was not in the original text but was added by the translators.

So, what Paul originally said in verse 4 is, "One's own house, well one that ruleth children having in subjection with all gravity."

⁵ [εἰ	δέ	τις	τοῦ	ἰδίου	οἴκου		προστῆναι	οὐκ	οἶδεν,	πῶς
if	(For	a man		his own	house,	how	to rule	not	know	how
1487	1161	5100	3588	2398	3624	<9999>	4291	3756	1492	4459
Ei	dé	tis	toú	idíou	oíkou		prosteénai	ouk	oíden	poós

	ἐκκλησίας	θεοῦ	ἐπιμελήσεται;],	
the	church	of God?)	shall he take care of	
9999	1577	2316	1959	
	ekkleesías	Theoú	epimeleésetai	

The word translated here as "a man" is the Greek word *tis.*

NT: 5100 *tis:* an enclitic indefinite pronoun; *some or any person* or object.

In the original language it says, "if (For any person's own house, how to rule not)."

The phrase "shall he take care of" is one word in the Greek:

NT:1959 *epimeleomai:* middle voice from NT:1909 and same as NT:3199; to care for (physically or otherwise).

There is nothing specifically masculine in that word.

So the words Paul wrote here are these: "if (For any person's own house, how to rule not know how the church of God?) shall take care of."

Nothing male or masculine in that verse at all.

6 μὴ	νεόφυτον,	ἵνα μὴ	τυφωθεὶς	εἰς		κρίμα	ἐμπέσῃ
Not	a novice,	lest	being lifted up with pride	into	the	condemnation	he fall
3361	3504	3363	5187	1519	9999	2917	1706
meé	neófuton	hína-meé	tufootheís	eis		kríma	empésee

τοῦ	διαβόλου.
of the	devil.
3588	1228
toú	diabólou

The words "he fall" is the Greek word NT:1706 *empipto,* from NT:1722 and NT:4098: "to fall on, i.e. (literally) to be trapped by, or (figuratively) be overwhelmed with."

There is nothing male or masculine specific about those words or in this verse in the original language.

So the words Paul wrote are these, "Not a novice, lest being lifted up with pride into condemnation to be trapped by the devil."

7	δεῖ	δὲ	καὶ	μαρτυρίαν	καλὴν	ἔχειν	ἀπὸ	τῶν	
he	must	Moreover		a report	good	have	of	them which	are
<9999>	1163	1161	2532	3141	2570	2192	575	3588	9999
	Deí	dé	kai	marturían	kaleén	échein	apó	toón	

ἔξωθεν,	ἵνα μὴ	εἰς	ὀνειδισμὸν	ἐμπέσῃ	καὶ		παγίδα	τοῦ	διαβόλου.
without;	lest	into	reproach	he fall	and	the	snare	of the	devil.
1855	2443 3361	1519	3680	1706	2532	9999	3803	3588	1228
éxoothen	hína meé	eis	oneidismón	empésee	kaí		pagída	toú	diabólou

That first word "he" in this verse is word 9999, which means what? It is not in the original text but was added by the translators.

That word translated "he fall" is the same one we looked at in verse 6, NT:1706, and we saw that there was nothing masculine or male in it.

So the words Paul wrote are these, "must Moreover a report good have of them which are without; lest into reproach fall and snare of the devil."

In verse 8, Paul starts giving the qualifications for a deacon.

What is a deacon? Seventeen out of the 21 times in the New Testament that Paul uses this word it is translated *minister*. Paul used that word to speak of himself and his ministry and the ministry of many of the other apostles.

8	Διακόνους	ὡσαύτως		σεμνούς,	μὴ	διλόγους,	μὴ	οἴνῳ
must the	deacons	Likewise	be	grave,	not	doubletongued,	not	wine,
9999	1249	5615	9999	4586	3361	1351	3361	3631
	Diakónous	hoosaútoos		semnoús	meé	dilógous	meé	oínoo

πολλῷ	προσέχοντας,	μὴ	αἰσχροκερδεῖς,
to much	given	not	greedy of filthy lucre;
4183	4337	3361	146
polloó	proséchontas	meé	aischrokerdeís

9	ἔχοντας	τὸ	μυστήριον	τῆς	πίστεως	ἐν	καθαρᾷ	συνειδήσει.
	Holding	the	mystery	of the	faith	in	pure	a conscience.
	2192	3588	3466	3588	4102	1722	2513	4893
	échontas	tó	musteérion	teés	písteoos	en	kathará	suneideései

10	καὶ	οὗτοι	δὲ	δοκιμαζέσθωσαν	πρῶτον,	εἶτα	διακονείτωσαν	
	also	these	And	let be proved;	first	then	let them use the office of a deacon,	found
	2532	3778	1161	1381	4412	1534	1247	9999
	Kaí	hoútoi	dé	dokimazésthoosan	proóton	eita	diakoneítoosan	

ἀνέγκλητοι	ὄντες.
blameless.	being
410	1510
anéngkleetoi	óntes

11	Γυναῖκας	ὡσαύτως		σεμνάς,	μὴ	διαβόλους,	νηφαλίους,	πιστὰς	ἐν
must their	wives	Even so	be	grave,	not	slanderers,	sober,	faithful	in
9999	1135	5615	9999	4586	3361	1228	3524	4103	1722
	Gunaíkas	hoosaútoos		semnás	meé	diabólous	neefalious	pistás	en

πᾶσιν.
all things.
3956
pásin

First of all, in verse 11 "must their" are 9999 words so they are not in the original text so let's eliminate those words.

The word translated "wives" is NT:1135, *gune:* "probably from the base of NT:1096; a woman; specially a wife."

So the words Paul wrote here are, "women even so grave, not slanderers, sober, faithful in all things."

There is nothing here that would disqualify women, only an admonition that the women deacons should be grave, not slanderers, sober, and faithful in all things.

¹²	διάκονοι	ἔστωσαν	μιᾶς	γυναικὸς		ἄνδρες,		τέκνων	καλῶς	προϊστάμενοι
the	deacons	Let be	of one	wife,	the	husbands	their	children	well.	ruling
9999	1249	2077	3391	1135	9999	435	9999	5043	2573	4291
	Diákonoi	éstoosan	miás	gunaikós		ándres		téknoon	kaloós	proistámenoi

καὶ	τῶν	ἰδίων	οἴκων.
and		their own	houses
2532	3588	2398	3624
kai	toón	idioon	oikoon

If we eliminate the extra words the translators added, the actual words Paul spoke here are, "Deacons, let be of one wife, husband children well, ruling and their own houses." Like the qualifications for a bishop in verse 2, this could easily be saying a male bishop should have only one wife, a female bishop should have only one husband.

¹³	οἱ	γὰρ	καλῶς	διακονήσαντες	βαθμὸν	ἑαυτοῖς	καλὸν	περιποιοῦνται
	they that	For	well	have used the office of a deacon	a degree,	to themselves	good	purchase
	3588	1063	2573	1247	898	1438	2570	4046
	Hoi	gár	kaloós	diakoneésantes	bathmón	heautois	kalón	peripoioúntai

καὶ	πολλὴν	παρρησίαν	ἐν		πίστει	τῇ		ἐν	Χριστῷ	Ἰησοῦ.
and	great	boldness	in	the	faith	which	is	in	Christ	Jesus.
2532	4183	3954	1722	9999	4102	3588	9999	1722	5547	2424
kai	polleén	parreesian	en		pistei	teé		en	Christoó	Ieesoú

Despite the interpreters of this passage adding masculine phrasing in the King James Version and other versions, the language used to enumerate the qualifications for leadership as both bishops and ministers here in 1 Timothy written by the apostle Paul is entirely gender-neutral. Paul chose his own words here and could have made these qualifications masculine and exclusively male had he chosen to do so. I think this is of great significance! If Paul had wanted to exclude women from leadership, he could have easily done so here, but he chose not to and intentionally chose to use gender-neutral language. So many do not know that Paul used gender-neutral language here because they have not taken the time to really look at this portion of scripture in-depth!

Let's look at Titus, where qualifications for ministry and leadership are again given.

For this cause left I thee in Crete, that thou shouldest set in order the things that are wanting, and ordain elders in every city, as I had appointed thee: if any be blameless, the husband of one wife, having faithful children not accused of riot or unruly. For a bishop must be blameless, as the steward of God; not selfwilled, not soon angry, not given to wine, no striker, not given to filthy lucre; but a lover of hospitality, a lover of good men, sober, just, holy, temperate; holding fast the faithful word as he hath been taught, that he may be able by sound doctrine both to exhort and to convince the gainsayers (Titus 1:5-9 KJV).

Let's look at it in the interlinear.

⁵ Τούτου	χάριν	ἀπέλιπόν	σε	ἐν	Κρήτῃ,	ἵνα	τὰ	λείποντα		
this	For cause	left I	thee	in	Crete,	that	the things	that are wanting,		
5127	5484	<620>	4571	1722	2914	2443	3588	3007		
Toútou	chárin	apélipón	se	en	Kreétee	hína	tá	leíponta		

ἐπιδιορθώσῃ	καὶ	καταστήσῃς	κατὰ	πόλιν	πρεσβυτέρους,	ὡς	ἐγώ
thou shouldest set in order	and	ordain	in every	city,	elders	as	I
1930	2532	2525	2596	4172	4245	5613	1473
epidiorthoósee	kai	katasteésees	katá	pólin	presbutérous	hoos	egoó

σοι	διεταξάμην,
thee:	had appointed
4671	1299
soi	dietaxámeen

Some think these elders are pastors; some think they are leaders of the governing body of the church. Regardless, it is Christian leadership in the church.

⁶ εἴ	τίς	ἐστιν	ἀνέγκλητος,	μιᾶς	γυναικὸς		ἀνήρ,	τέκνα	ἔχων
If any	be		blameless,	of one	wife,	the	husband	children	having
1536	2076		410	3391	1135	9999	435	5043	2192
eí-tis	estin	anéngkleetos	miás	gunaikós		aneér	tékna	échoon

πιστά,	μὴ	ἐν κατηγορίᾳ	ἀσωτίας	ἤ	ἀνυπότακτα.	
faithful	not	accused	of riot	or	unruly.	
4103	3361	1722 2724	810	2228	506	
pistá	meé	en kateegoría	asootías	eé	anupótakta	

Again, the word *the* in "the husband" is not in the original text. It is literally one wife, husband signifying it could be either one wife of one husband or one husband of one wife. The significance of this verse seems to be the fidelity to one's marriage vows, not the gender of the elder.

⁷ δεῖ	γὰρ	τὸν	ἐπίσκοπον	ἀνέγκλητον	εἶναι	ὡς	θεοῦ	οἰκονόμον,
must	For	a	bishop	blameless,	be	as	of God;	the steward
1163	1063	3588	1985	410	1511	5613	2316	9999 <3623>
Deí	gár	tón	epískopon	anéngkleeton	eínai	hoos	Theoú	oikonómon

μὴ	αὐθάδη,	μὴ	ὀργίλον,	μὴ	πάροινον,	μὴ	πλήκτην,	μὴ
not	selfwilled,	not	soon angry,	not	given to wine,	no	striker,	not
3361	829	3361	3711	3361	3943	3361	4131	3361
meé	authádee	meé	orgilon	meé	pároinon	meé	pleékteen	meé

αἰσχροκερδῆ,
given to filthy lucre;
146
aischrokerdeé

⁸ ἀλλὰ	φιλόξενον	φιλάγαθον		σώφρονα	δίκαιον	ὅσιον
But	a lover of hospitality,	a lover of good	men,	sober,	just,	holy,
235	5382	5358	9999	4998	1342	3741
allá	filóxenon	filágathon		soófrona	díkaion	hósion

ἐγκρατῆ,
temperate;
1468
engkrateé

I think it is interesting that the translators added the word *men* here in verse 8 when it is not in the original text. It is a 9999 word. Without it, this verse says a bishop must be a lover of good, which seems like a better translation than a lover of good men.

⁹ ἀντεχόμενον	τοῦ	κατὰ	τὴν	διδαχὴν	πιστοῦ	λόγου,	ἵνα
Holding fast	the	as		he hath been taught,	faithful	word	that
472	3588	2596	3588	1322	4103	3056	2443
antechómenon	toú	katá	teén	didacheén	pistoú	lógou	hína

δυνατὸς	ᾖ	καὶ	παρακαλεῖν	ἐν	τῇ	διδασκαλίᾳ	τῇ	ὑγιαινούσῃ
able	he may be	both	to exhort	by		doctrine		sound
1415	5600	2532	3870	1722	3588	1319	3588	5198
dunatós	eé	kaí	parakaleín	en	teé	didaskalía	teé	hugiainoúsee

καὶ	τοὺς	ἀντιλέγοντας	ἐλέγχειν.
and	the	gainsayers.	to convince
2532	3588	483	1651
kaí	toús	antilégontas	eléngchein

That phrase "as he hath been taught" is Greek word NT:1322 *didache*, from NT:1321: "instruction (the act or the matter)."

There is nothing masculine or male about that word; the translators just added the word *he*.

That phrase "he may be" is Greek word NT:5600, "including the oblique forms, as well *ases* (ace); e (ay); etc.; the subjunctive of NT:1510; (may, might, can, could, would, should, must, etc.; also with NT:1487 and it's comparative, as well as other particles) be."

There is a lot of stuff there, none of which has anything to do with being male.

Paul, in giving the qualifications of leaders in the early church for bishops, pastors, deacons, and elders, intentionally chose to use exclusively gender-neutral language. Nothing here says this is for the male gender only or that females are in any way excluded. In fact, he intentionally used gender-inclusive language so that the qualifications are open to both men and women and both men and women are qualified to lead by the content of their character, not by their gender.

In Paul's qualifications for Christian ministry and leadership, in the Greek it says one wife, husband. But if you are going to say that Paul was strictly saying that all leaders in the Christian church *must* be the husband of one wife, then Paul is eliminating himself from Christian leadership because he never married and is therefore *not* the husband of one wife. Paul would also be eliminating Jesus from Christian leadership because He never married either. No. That is not what Paul meant. Most theologians agree that Paul is referring to being monogamous if you are in a marriage relationship, not being in a polygamous relationship, and not being one who cheats on one's spouse.

Paul intentionally choosing gender-neutral language in his qualifications for ministry and leadership is simply more proof that despite some people's belief to the contrary, Paul was a champion for women ministers.

In 1 Corinthians 14, Paul is talking about people using their vocal gifts in the church. He is trying to bring order to that which is out of order. Let's take a look at it as he enumerates who may use their vocal gifts in the church service.

> *How is it then, brethren? when ye come together, every one of you hath a psalm, hath a doctrine, hath a tongue, hath a revelation, hath an interpretation. Let all things be done unto edifying (1 Corinthians 14:26 KJV).*

That word *brethren* there, while seemingly masculine, is often used by Paul to address all Christians when he is teaching. For example in Romans 12:1 it says:

> *I beseech you therefore, brethren, by the mercies of God, that ye present your bodies a living sacrifice, holy, acceptable unto God, which is your reasonable service. And be not conformed to this world: but be ye transformed by the renewing of your*

mind, that ye may prove what is that good, and acceptable, and perfect, will of God (Romans 12:1-2 KJV).

Is this a teaching that only male believers have to follow because it says "brethren"? No. Obviously, it is instruction given to all believers both male and female. If you try to say that everywhere Paul used the word *brethren* only applies to males, then a *lot* of Paul's instruction in the New Testament would not have to be followed by women. We know that is not the case. He is referring to the brotherhood of all believers, both male and female.

How is it then, brethren? when ye come together, every one of you hath a psalm, hath a doctrine, hath a tongue, hath a revelation, hath an interpretation. Let all things be done unto edifying (1 Corinthians 14:26 KJV).

I want you to notice that Paul says *every one of you,* which is certainly gender-inclusive language. He says *every one of you* hath a psalm, hath a doctrine, hath a tongue, hath a revelation, hath an interpretation.

If any man speak in an unknown tongue, let it be by two, or at the most by three, and that by course; and let one interpret (1 Corinthians 14:27 KJV).

In verse 27, that word *man* there is the Greek word *tis,* which means anyone.

But if there be no interpreter, let him keep silence in the church; and let him speak to himself, and to God (1 Corinthians 14:28 KJV).

The masculine words *him or himself* are used three times in the King James Version here in verse 28 but those words are not in the original language.

The phrase "let him keep silence" is the Greek word *sigato,* which means to keep silent, but has nothing to do with being male or masculine.

The phrase in verse 28 "let him speak" is the Greek word *laleo,* which means to talk, i.e. utter words, and it has nothing to do with being male; the word *him* was just added by the translators.

The phrase "to himself" is the Greek word *heautou* and is an obsolete word which could be translated "himself, herself or thine own self." There is nothing specifically male about it.

Let the prophets speak two or three, and let the other judge. If any thing be revealed to another that sitteth by, let the first hold his peace. For ye may all prophesy one by one, that all may learn, and all may be comforted (1 Corinthians 14:29-31 KJV).

Who may prophesy? He said you may *all* prophesy.

Again, you can see that Paul intentionally used gender-inclusive language in these verses.

We will look at the rest of 1 Corinthians 14 where Paul specifically addresses women in Chapter 10.

CHAPTER 9

"LET THE WOMAN LEARN IN SILENCE"

We can clearly see from the things we have studied thus far that all through the scriptures, women were created to stand equal with men in rulership and dominion over the earth and over the enemy. We see that *even after the fall,* God chose and appointed and anointed women to be in ministry and to lead both spiritually and naturally.

We looked at Jesus' interactions with women both before and after His death, burial, and resurrection. We looked at prophecies which foretold of women being used along with men in the great spiritual outpouring of the "last days," which scripture says began on the day of Pentecost.

We looked at Paul's interactions with women and determined that Paul was not only *not* against women in ministry but he was a champion of women using their gifts in church meetings, even their vocal gifts.

We looked at the qualifications for ministry and leadership in ministry as outlined by Paul and saw that the verbiage Paul used was totally gender-neutral and was 100 percent based on character and not gender.

In this chapter, we are going to tackle some of the "tough" verses Paul wrote, which on their surface seem to eliminate women from ministry. I am going to need you to put aside your preconceived notions of what these scriptures say and open your mind and heart to hear what the scriptures actually do say.

In 2 Peter 3:16, Peter said he found some of the things Paul said in the epistles hard to understand. If they were hard for Peter to understand, we can easily see how hard it is for us some 2,000 years later to understand what was going on so long ago that made Paul say some of the things he did. While the people he was writing to were familiar with the problems Paul was addressing, we are left trying to piece together what we can from our knowledge of the Word as a whole and from history to understand what was going on and what he was trying to say in these passages.

So, let's jump in.

Let the woman learn in silence with all subjection. But I suffer not a woman to teach, nor to usurp authority over the man, but to be in silence. For Adam was first formed, then Eve. And Adam was not deceived, but the woman being deceived was in the transgression. Notwithstanding she shall be saved in childbearing, if they continue in faith and charity and holiness with sobriety (1 Timothy 2:11-15 KJV).

At first glance, this is pretty harsh and straightforward verbiage. But let's look deeper because it seems on the surface to contradict other clear scripture where Paul allows women to use their gifts, even their vocal gifts in church. And it contradicts him allowing women to be ministers, which we know he did.

So, when the scripture seems to contradict itself then there is something we are not properly interpreting.

Whenever we have trouble properly interpreting a portion of scripture then one of our most basic rules of Bible interpretation comes into play. That is, a scripture must be interpreted in context, meaning in its setting—its chapter and book, other books by the same writer, its testament, and even the Bible as a whole. If you are unclear on a verse's meaning, first, back up and read what the writer is talking about before they come to this portion of scripture, then read on after the verses in question to see what comes after, to see if the writer's words before and after the verses in question clarify a verse's meaning.

We need to look at the context of these verses to help us understand what they are truly saying.

The thing that Paul was trying to combat in this whole book of the Bible is false doctrine being taught at the church in Ephesus. Paul was telling Timothy that he must get under control the wrong doctrine being taught. The theme of correcting wrong doctrine is all throughout this book.

*Paul, an apostle of Jesus Christ by the commandment of God our Saviour, and Lord Jesus Christ, which is our hope; unto Timothy, my own son in the faith: Grace, mercy, and peace, from God our Father and Jesus Christ our Lord. As I besought thee to abide still at Ephesus, when I went into Macedonia, **that thou mightest charge some that they teach no other doctrine, neither give heed to fables and endless genealogies, which minister questions, rather than godly edifying which is in faith:** so do. Now the end of the commandment is charity out of a pure heart, and of a good conscience, and of faith unfeigned: from which **some having swerved have turned aside unto vain jangling; desiring*** *to be teachers of the law; understanding neither what they say, nor whereof they affirm (1 Timothy 1:1-7 KJV).*

Now the Spirit speaketh expressly, that in the latter times some shall depart from the faith, giving heed to seducing spirits, and doctrines of devils; speaking lies in hypocrisy; having their conscience seared with a hot iron (1 Timothy 4:1-2 KJV).

If **thou put the brethren in remembrance of these things,** *thou shalt be a good minister of Jesus Christ,* **nourished up in the words of faith and of good doctrine,** *whereunto thou hast attained. But* **refuse profane and old wives' fables,** *and exercise thyself rather unto godliness (1 Timothy 4:6-7 KJV).*

Take heed unto thyself, and unto the doctrine; continue in them: for in doing this thou shalt both save thyself, and them that hear thee *(1 Timothy 4:16 KJV).*

If any man teach otherwise, and consent not to wholesome words, even the words of our Lord Jesus Christ, and to the doctrine which is according to godliness; he is proud, knowing nothing, but doting about questions and strifes of words, whereof cometh envy, strife, railings, evil surmisings, perverse disputings of men of corrupt minds, and destitute of the truth, supposing that gain is godliness: from such withdraw thyself *(1 Timothy 6:3-5 KJV).*

O Timothy, keep that which is committed to thy trust, **avoiding profane and vain babblings, and oppositions of science falsely so called: which some professing have erred**

concerning the faith. *Grace be with thee. Amen (1 Timothy 6:20-21 KJV).*

The thing that Paul was trying to combat in this whole book was the false doctrine being taught at the church in Ephesus. He was telling Timothy he must get under control the wrong doctrine being taught. That admonition is all through this book.

So with that background, let's look again at the verses in question.

Let the woman learn in silence with all subjection (1 Timothy 2:11 KJV).

Let the woman do what? *Learn.*

In this verse Paul was not talking about a woman teaching, but in this verse he was dealing with how women are behaving while trying to *learn* something at church.

That word *silence* there doesn't mean saying nothing. The word for being totally silent and saying nothing is *sigato,* but that is not the word used in this verse.

The word translated here "in silence" is NT:2271, *hesuchia:* "feminine of NT:2272; (as noun) *stillness,* i.e. *desistance from bustle or language."*

It says it is the feminine of NT:2272, *hesuchios:* "a prolonged form of a compound probably a derivative of the base of NT:1476 and perhaps NT:2192; properly, *keeping one's seat (sedentary),* i.e. *(by implication) still (undisturbed, undisturbing)."*

In essence what Paul was saying is, "Let the women learn in stillness, desisting from bustle or speaking out. They are to keep their seat, be sedentary, undisturbed, and not disturbing others."

We don't know what all these women were doing to disrupt the church service while trying to learn, but it was egregious enough that Paul felt the need to address it, and basically he was telling them to settle down.

Really, this is how everyone who is learning should conduct themselves. It was obviously more of a problem for these women in the first century then the men just because they really didn't know how to act in church because they weren't allowed in public assemblies before, due to their culture.

Some people believe men and women were seated in different areas of the church. In some nations I have visited, it is that way to this day—men sit on one side of the church, women on the other. Perhaps they were calling out to their spouses asking questions or just calling out their questions.

Maybe.

But there is something else I want you to see here in verse 11.

Let the woman learn in silence with all subjection (1 Timothy 2:11 KJV).

The word *woman* here is singular, not plural. Earlier Paul refers to both men and women in the plural, but why here does he refer to *a woman*, not women?

In verse 12 the word *woman* is also singular.

But I suffer not a woman to teach, nor to usurp authority over the man, but to be in silence (1 Timothy 2:12 KJV).

Let's look at this in the Young's Literal Translation.

And a woman I do not suffer to teach, nor to rule a husband, but to be in quietness (1 Timothy 2:12 YLT).

Because the word *woman* is singular, some believe that Paul was talking about a specific problem woman and all of this is directed at that one woman and not at women at large.

Maybe.

But I think there are other possible explanations here too. First, we need to look at the predominant religion in that area at that time, which was the worship of the goddess Artemis of the Ephesians or Diana as she is also called.

Artemis is considered the "great mother goddess" and the source of life, and her temple was run entirely by female officials. There are statues of this goddess that have been found by archeologists that depict her with a crown on her head, signifying the people believed her to be the great goddess in charge of life. She had a chain of eggs around her midsection as she was also regarded as the goddess of fertility. It was she, they thought, you had to worship to have children and for women to be protected through the birth process. Giving birth today is a struggle for many, and I would imagine that approaching it in the first century without all our technology would have caused many women who did not know the truth to call on this false goddess to protect them through the process of childbirth.

As these followers of Artemis got born again and came into the church, it is very likely that they brought their pagan beliefs into the church and could have been mixing this false religion with their Christianity until they had the opportunity to be thoroughly taught the truth.

I believe some of their wrong teaching is what Paul sought to correct here.

Let's look at it again.

But I suffer not a woman to teach, nor to usurp authority over the man, but to be in silence (1 Timothy 2:12 KJV).

Now we know that Paul wasn't against women teaching and preaching the Word. It was done even here in Ephesus, which is where Timothy was when Paul wrote him this letter.

And a certain Jew named Apollos, born at Alexandria, an eloquent man, and mighty in the scriptures, came to Ephesus. This man was instructed in the way of the Lord; and being fervent in the spirit, he spake and taught diligently the things of the Lord, knowing only the baptism of John. And he began to speak boldly in the synagogue: whom when Aquila and Priscilla had heard, they took him unto them, and expounded unto him the way of God more perfectly (Acts 18:24-26 KJV).

I want you to see that right here in Ephesus, both Priscilla and Aquila pulled Apollos, a man, aside and taught him the way more accurately. Nowhere does it say that the leadership had an objection to this and Priscilla shouldn't have been teaching Apollos because he is a man and she is a woman.

The great female minister Priscilla along with her husband Aquila were working in the Ephesian church off and on throughout their ministry.

I think that to understand 1 Timothy 2:12, we need to understand the word translated here "nor" as it brings further light on this subject.

The word is NT:3761, *oude,* from NT:3756 and NT:1161, "not however, i.e. neither, nor, not even."

In 1 Timothy 2:12 the conjunction *oude* joins *didaskein* ("to teach") with the Greek word *authentein.*

I heard Rick Renner and other Greek scholars say that in the Greek language, that word *oude* ties the two parts of that sentence into one thought.

So those are not two separate thoughts—I do not allow a woman to teach and I do not allow a woman to usurp authority over a man. They are tied together by that word *nor,* or *oude* in the Greek, and that word ties those two sentences into one thought. This verse could easily be interpreted, "I do not allow a woman to teach that women are dominant over men" or "I do not allow a woman to teach for the purpose of dominating a man."

Let's look at the word translated "usurp authority" in this verse. It is the Greek word *authentein,* NT: 831, *authenteo*: "from a compound of NT:846 and an obsolete *hentes* (a worker); to act of oneself, i.e. (figuratively) dominate."

This is a very odd word that Paul used here, and it is the only time this word is used in the Bible. There are 12 other Greek words used for exercising authority in the New Testament, but Paul doesn't use any of those; he uses this very obscure Greek word.

The original meaning of this word Paul used here was to murder with one's own hands. This is a violent, aggressive word with a very negative meaning. It meant to dominate but in an aggressive, violent way. This verse could easily be interpreted, "I do not allow a woman in her teaching to advocate the overthrowing of authority by force."

Over time it came to be used for originating something with one's own hand, like "I authored a book." *Author,* from *authentein*—or our word *authentic,* which means "from one's own self."

This verse could very easily be interpreted, "I do not allow a woman to proclaim herself author of a man or the originator of a man while teaching."

That interpretation would directly refute the wrong teachings of the day from Artemis.

But I suffer not a woman to teach, nor to usurp authority over the man, but to be in silence (1 Timothy 2:12 KJV).

The last phrase of that verse "but to be in silence" once again uses the word *hesuchia,* which *doesn't* mean to be silent, but it means to be still, desistance from bustle or speaking out, keeping one's seat, being sedentary, not disturbed, and not disturbing others. The full breakdown of that word is found in the prior pages of this chapter pertaining to verse 11.

Basically, he was saying that women "need to settle down, stop causing a disturbance in church, and they need to stop advocating for an overthrowing of authority in their teaching" or that women "need to settle down, stop causing a disturbance in church and stop teaching this false doctrine that women are the author or originator of the man and dominant over him."

For Adam was first formed, then Eve (1 Timothy 2:13 KJV).

I believe he recounted the creation account here to further refute the false doctrine of Artemis that women were created first and were the author or originator of the man.

I don't believe that he was using this to imply dominance of men over women due to creation order as I have heard it taught. If creation order strictly sets dominance, then men are to be led by and dominated by any and every animal that was ever created—frogs, lizards, etc.—as *all* the animals were created before Adam.

> *And Adam was not deceived, but the woman being deceived was in the transgression (1 Timothy 2:14 KJV).*

When I casually read the Word, this always hit me as Paul being smug, saying the man was better than the woman because he wasn't deceived, but it was the woman who sinned. But that cannot be the proper interpretation because Adam sinned too. If he wasn't deceived then he simply knowingly chose to harden his heart toward God and intentionally chose to sin by disobeying God. That is in no way better than Eve, and in fact, it is worse.

As I have studied, I think this verse is once again refuting the wrong doctrine of Artemis that was sneaking into the church with the converts who had yet to learn enough truth to refute the lies they had been taught in the worship of Artemis.

Women were not the perfect, never-failing deities that the worship of Artemis portrayed. No, Eve was deceived and fell into transgression. That is true. She is not perfect or unfailing. She is just as fallible as Adam, and in fact, in Genesis we see that she fell into sin first—but then Adam followed right after her.

Ultimately, they *both* sinned, as have all of humanity since then.

> *For **all** have sinned, and come short of the glory of God (Romans 3:23 KJV).*

If I were allowed to add the words "with him" to the end of that sentence in 1 Timothy 2:14, I believe you would come to the proper interpretation.

And Adam was not deceived, but the woman being deceived was in the transgression [with him] *(1 Timothy 2:14 KJV).*

Of course, I can't add those words as no one can add to the scriptures, but we know they both sinned, and I believe Paul said what he said to refute the false doctrine of Artemis. Women were not the perfect, never-failing deities that the worship of Artemis portrayed.

Notwithstanding she shall be saved in childbearing, if they continue in faith and charity and holiness with sobriety (1 Timothy 2:15 KJV).

Though that word *saved* in this sentence is *sozo* in the Greek, we know Paul is not referring to the salvation of our souls, which causes us to be born again. Romans 10:9-10 lays out the only way to the salvation of our souls as believing in your heart and speaking your faith out of your mouth.

That if thou shalt confess with thy mouth the Lord Jesus, and shalt believe in thine heart that God hath raised him from the dead, thou shalt be saved. For with the heart man believeth unto righteousness; and with the mouth confession is made unto salvation (Romans 10:9-10 KJV).

That is the *only* way to save your soul and be born again, so what is Paul talking about?

I believe this scripture is saying that Christian women shall be saved or protected through the difficulties of childbirth if they continue in faith and charity and holiness with sobriety.

That word *sozo* translated in verse 15 as "saved" is NT: 4982, *sozo*: "from a primary *sos* (contraction for obsolete *saoz*, *"safe"*), to save, i.e. deliver or protect (literally or figuratively)."

I believe Paul was assuring the new converts from the pagan religion that they do not need to call on or sacrifice to the goddess Artemis or Diana to get through childbirth, that they will now be saved through childbirth by their faith in Christ as they continue to walk in love and live holy, self-controlled lives.

There is absolutely nothing here in 1 Timothy 2 saying that women are not allowed to teach at all and need to be totally silent and are forbidden to speak at all in church. Rather, in their attempt to *learn* and be taught in church, they need to be careful keep their seats and not create a disturbance in the service. Those women who teach are not to teach for the purpose of advocating an overthrowing of authority, nor are they to teach the false doctrine that they were taught in the worship of Artemis about women being created first and being the source of men's creation. They also need to understand that Eve did sin; she was not the perfect, infallible creature that the worship of Artemis teaches. It also is an admonition that women no longer have to serve Artemis to have children and to be protected during the process of childbirth.

CHAPTER 10

"IT IS NOT PERMITTED UNTO THEM TO SPEAK"

Let your women keep silence in the churches: for it is not permitted unto them to speak; but they are commanded to be under obedience as also saith the law. And if they will learn any thing, let them ask their husbands at home: for it is a shame for women to speak in the church. What? came the word of God out from you? or came it unto you only? If any man think himself to be a prophet, or spiritual, let him acknowledge that the things that I write unto you are the commandments of the Lord. But if any man be ignorant, let him be ignorant (1 Corinthians 14:34-38 KJV).

We need to look at the context of these verses to help us understand what they are truly saying.

If we backed all the way up to the beginning of chapter 14, we would see that in this chapter, Paul is setting things in order in the Corinthian church that are out of order. He talks about not just getting up in the pulpit and speaking in tongues for a sermon and also about people talking over each other while trying to share, etc. In this whole chapter he is talking about things being done decently and in order in the church.

So, let's back up and give these verses some context.

*How is it then, brethren? when ye come together, every one of you hath a psalm, hath a doctrine, hath a tongue, hath a revelation, hath an interpretation. Let all things be done unto edifying. If any man speak in an unknown tongue, let it be by two, or at the most by three, and that by course; and let one interpret. But if there be no interpreter, let him keep silence in the church; and let him speak to himself, and to God. Let the prophets speak two or three, and let the other judge. If any thing be revealed to another that sitteth by, let the first hold his peace. For ye may all prophesy one by one, that all may learn, and all may be comforted. And the spirits of the prophets are subject to the prophets. For God is not the author of confusion, but of peace, as in all churches of the saints. **Let your women keep silence in the churches: for it is not permitted unto them to speak; but they are commanded to be under obedience as also saith the law. And if they will learn any thing, let them ask their husbands at home: for it is a shame for women to speak in the church.** What? came the word of God out from you? or came it unto you only? If any man think himself to be a prophet, or spiritual, let him acknowledge that the things that I write unto you are the commandments of the Lord. But if any man be ignorant, let him be ignorant. Wherefore, brethren, covet to prophesy, and forbid not to speak with tongues. Let all things be done decently and in order (1 Corinthians 14:26-40 KJV).*

You can clearly see here, he is talking about order and things being done decently and in order in the church.

This chapter is odd because it is the only portion of the scriptures where some verses, verses 34 and 35 specifically (in bold, above), move around in some of the early manuscripts of the Bible. This is the only place I know where the verses are in a different order when you compare one early manuscript with another. The different order of the verses has caused some to speculate that those two verses were a marginal note or commentary added by someone that somehow found its way into the actual text of the scripture. It has caused some to question whether those verses were actually supposed to be in this text at all.

Personally, I would never do anything that would undermine the veracity of scripture and, therefore, I am not taking that stance.

However, if we move verses 34 and 35 to the other place it was found in early manuscripts (which is after verse 40), then it does take a lot of the harshness out of those scriptures.

Let's back up to verse 29 and run into it moving those scriptures to the end of the chapter just so you can see what I am talking about.

Let the prophets speak two or three, and let the other judge. If any thing be revealed to another that sitteth by, let the first hold his peace. For ye may all prophesy one by one, that all may learn, and all may be comforted. And the spirits of the prophets are subject to the prophets. For God is not the author of confusion, but of peace, as in all churches of the saints (1 Corinthians 14:29-33 KJV).

What? came the word of God out from you? or came it unto you only? If any man think himself to be a prophet, or spiritual, let him acknowledge that the things that I write unto you are the commandments of the Lord. But if any man be ignorant, let him be ignorant. Wherefore, brethren, covet to prophesy, and forbid not to speak with tongues. Let all things be done decently and in order (1 Corinthians 14:36-40 KJV).

Let your women keep silence in the churches: for it is not permitted unto them to speak; but they are commanded to be under obedience as also saith the law. And if they will learn any thing, let them ask their husbands at home: for it is a shame for women to speak in the church (1 Corinthians 14:34-35 KJV).

Placing those verses there does take a lot of the harshness out of the scripture. I don't think it has done any damage to the scriptures for those verses to be put in either place, but I am not willing to undermine the veracity of the scriptures as we have them. So let's put those verses back in the place we found them (as verses 34 and 35), and let's see if we can figure out what Paul is talking about.

First of all, I want to repeat what we already know, and that is in this chapter, Paul is setting order in the church.

Now let's look specifically at the two verses we are trying to understand.

Let your women keep silence in the churches: for it is not permitted unto them to speak; but they are commanded to be under obedience as also saith the law. And if they will learn any thing, let them ask their husbands at home: for it is a shame for women to speak in the church (1 Corinthians 14:34-35 KJV).

The first thing I want you to notice here in verse 35 is that the problem Paul is seeking to address here and put in order is how women are endeavoring to *learn* at church that is out of order and causing things not to be done decently and in order in the Corinthian church.

*I want you to notice the problem is **not** that a woman tried to get up and teach. The problem is in how the women were trying to **learn**.* In trying to *learn*, they were doing something that was out of order and disrupting the service.

If they would *learn anything*, let them ask their husbands at home. Why would he say that? There was something about the way they were trying to learn that was disruptive to the service. Obviously, it had to do with them speaking out. As Paul ties those two thoughts together, he admonishes them to ask their husbands what they want to learn or understand when they get home. Paul says the answer to the problem of the women speaking in church was for them to ask their husbands at home to explain what they were trying to understand or learn.

And if they will learn any thing, let them ask their husbands at home: for it is a shame for women to speak in the church (1 Corinthians 14:35 KJV).

We know that Paul is not against women using their vocal gifts in church, generally speaking. In this same book over in chapter 11, he gives the decorum necessary for when women use their vocal gifts in the public service.

And any woman who [publicly] prays or prophesies (teaches, refutes, reproves, admonishes, or comforts) when she is bareheaded

dishonors her head (her husband); it is the same as [if her head
were] shaved (1 Corinthians 11:5 AMPC).

So why did Paul say what he said in chapter 14 verses 34 and
35?

Again, I see nothing in these verses that says the problem Paul
is addressing is women getting up and trying to teach. These verses
clearly say the problem was in the disruptive way the women
were trying to learn.

Some theologians believe that men sat in one area of the
building and women in another and the women were calling
out to their husbands asking questions right in the middle of the
service.

That could be it. Women were untrained in public meetings
and the etiquette of those meetings and perhaps did not know
how to conduct themselves properly while trying to learn.

Another theory is that it has to do with the predominant
religion in Corinth before Christianity, which was the worship
of Bacchus. When people get born again in totally unreached
areas, it may take them a while to unlearn what they were taught
in their false religions, and sometimes those wrong things followed them over into the church until they were fully taught the
truth.

Bacchus was known as the god of drinking and revelry, a
party god, if you will. In fact, a drunken orgy is still called a
bacchanalia to this day. Bacchus was portrayed as a liberator and
during his follower's drunken frenzies, he was thought to "loosen"
the tongue of those who partake of intoxicating beverages giving people the freedom to say and do whatever they want. There
were whole segments and festivals of that religion just for women.

So, while worshipping Bacchus, they would drink and get drunk and whip themselves into a frenzy until they were free enough to just say and do anything they wanted.

Well, if that same theory of "when I am under the influence of my deity, I can just let my mouth fly" invaded the church, you can easily see how that could be a problematic disruption.

We know from 1 Corinthians 11 that some were getting drunk on the communion wine, probably another influence from Bacchus creeping into the church.

That could be it—we don't know exactly what those women were doing while trying to learn. I do want you to see that however they were trying to learn, they were doing it in a way that was disrupting the service; that disruption of the service was the thing that needed to be put in order.

To me, there are so many fascinating things about this chapter and these verses.

Let's look at it.

Let your women keep silence in the churches: for it is not permitted unto them to speak; but they are commanded to be under obedience as also saith the law (1 Corinthians 14:34 KJV).

I and a lot of theologians find the second part of this verse puzzling for several reasons.

1. When has Paul ever commanded New Testament believers to keep the law? So, to whose law was he referring? The law of Moses? The laws of Rome? We just don't know.

2. Every other time when Paul mentions the Old Testament law, he quotes the passage to which he is referring. He does not do that here.

3. I have found nothing in the law of Moses that says a woman must be under obedience, and certainly, I have not found anything in there that says women are not allowed to speak in church.

Beyond that, there is something here in verse 34 I really want you to see.

The word *silence* in that verse is Strong's NT:4601, *sigao*: "from NT:4602; to keep silent (transitively or intransitively)."

Most of us were taught that means women have been given a permanent injunction against *ever* speaking in church, but that is not how that word is used.

That same word is used two other times right here in chapter 14.

How is it then, brethren? when ye come together, every one of you hath a psalm, hath a doctrine, hath a tongue, hath a revelation, hath an interpretation. Let all things be done unto edifying. If any man speak in an unknown tongue, let it be by two, or at the most by three, and that by course; and let one interpret. But if there be no interpreter, let him keep silence in the church; and let him speak to himself, and to God (1 Corinthians 14:26-28 KJV).

The Greek word translated "let him keep silence" in verse 28 is the same word used in verse 34 about women keeping silence. It is Strong's 4601 *sigao*. We don't interpret it here in verse

28 as a permanent injunction against those who are speaking in tongues in church, but we interpret it as being silent only *in that moment to keep order* if there is no interpreter.

> *Let the prophets speak two or three, and let the other judge. If any thing be revealed to another that sitteth by, let the first hold his peace (1 Corinthians 14:29-30 KJV).*

The Greek word translated here in verse 30 as "hold his peace" is the same word used in verse 34 about women keeping silence. It is Strong's 4601 *sigao.* We don't interpret it here in verse 30 as a permanent injunction against those who are prophesying in church, but we interpret it as being silent only in this moment to keep order if there is another upon whom the Spirit moves.

So, why do we interpret that same exact word differently in verse 34? In verse 34 it is taken as a permanent injunction against women *ever* speaking in church instead of only being an injunction to *momentarily be quiet* to address a specific circumstance of disorder like it is in verses 28 and 30.

In this chapter, Paul is clearly talking about keeping order in a church service. In verses 28 and 30 he is making the point that sometimes we have to temporarily be quiet and hold our peace just for this moment to maintain order in certain circumstances. In verses 28 and 30, it is clearly not an injunction against prophets and those speaking in tongues being permanently barred from speaking in church *ever again,* so why would we consider the exact same word used in verse 34 as saying women are permanently barred from speaking in church?

I think Paul was saying the same thing in verses 28, 30, and 34. In certain circumstances when things are out of order, we may all need to hold our peace for this moment so that things are done in order.

That word *sigao* or *sigato* is used 10 times in the New Testament, and *every* time it means to temporarily be quiet because of the specific circumstances of the moment. *Never* is it a permanent injunction against someone ever speaking again.

In verses 34 and 35 there was something about the way the women were trying to learn in the Corinthian church that was causing them to speak out of turn and it caused disorder. Paul was trying to stop that particular circumstance of disruptive behavior in the church service. He was not forbidding women from teaching or using their vocal gifts in the church service.

That is consistent with what Paul told the women in Ephesus about how they were to learn too—being still, desisting from bustle or speaking out, keeping one's seat, being sedentary, not disturbed, and not disturbing others.

CHAPTER 11

HOW DID WE GET HERE?

Why does the enemy work so hard against women? For so long he has caused the portions of scripture regarding women to be misinterpreted, and he has intentionally diminished women both in their own sight and in society's sight for millennia. But why?

I think there are several reasons.

1. I believe it goes back to the garden and the enmity God said there would be between the woman and the serpent, Satan.

And the Lord God said unto the serpent, Because thou hast done this, thou art cursed above all cattle, and above every beast of the field; upon thy belly shalt thou go, and dust shalt thou eat all the days of thy life: **and I will put enmity between thee and the woman,** *and between thy seed and her seed; it shall bruise thy head, and thou shalt bruise his heel (Genesis 3:14-15 KJV).*

The Lord said clear back in Genesis 3 that there would be enmity between the woman and the snake, Satan.

I looked that word *enmity* up on my Merriam-Webster dictionary app on my phone, and it says enmity is "active and typically mutual hatred or ill will."

The fall left women as mortal enemies of Satan. Make no mistake, Satan hates every child of God, both male and female, but there was and is particular animosity between him and the woman.

That is understandable when we read the rest of this verse.

And I will put enmity between thee and the woman, and between thy seed and her seed; it shall bruise thy head, and thou shalt bruise his heel (Genesis 3:15 KJV).

In the New International Version it says this:

And I will put enmity between you and the woman, and between your offspring and hers; **he will crush your head,** *and you will strike his heel (Genesis 3:15 NIV).*

God promised the snake, Satan, that the offspring of the woman would crush his head. No wonder he particularly hates women.

This, of course, was fulfilled by Jesus. I believe every time a believer uses his or her authority and enforces the fact that Satan's head or authority is crushed, he relives his defeat.

The fact that this crushing of his head by Jesus was already accomplished hasn't diminished his hatred one bit. In fact, Revelation says his fury is great because he knows his time is short.

Therefore rejoice, you heavens and you who dwell in them! But woe to the earth and the sea, because the devil has gone down to you! He is filled with fury, because he knows that his time is short (Revelation 12:12 NIV).

His fury is directed at both men and women, and that makes us need each other even more. We need to fight for each other, not against each other. We need to fight against the powers of darkness that would try to steal, kill, and destroy either one of us!

2. I believe the fall has also had a negative effect on some men, with Satan twisting the words that God spoke to men (husbands) about leadership, into a need for some to dominate and conquer rather than love, protect, and lead. Of course, that is not true of *all* men, but it is true of some.

3. In causing people to think that women are not allowed to minister, it eliminates 50 percent of the spiritual workforce as the human population is nearly evenly split between men and women.

Satan is not stupid, and he thinks he has found a way to eliminate 50 percent of the spiritual workforce. In most of the world, there are 50 percent fewer people sharing the gospel, plundering hell, and populating heaven because they haven't understood what the Bible truly says about women.

CHAPTER 12

FREE TO ANSWER HIS CALL

My goal in writing this book is to free women to see themselves the way *God* sees them and to show them from the Word what God says about them so that they can respond if He should ask them to step out and do something for Him.

I also wanted to encourage everyone, men and women alike, to do what the Bible says we should do. We are to *study* the Word of God to see what the scriptures actually say and not just be superficial and surface in our reading. We also cannot just accept what someone else has told us that it says. We are responsible before God to study and to get it right!

I would also like to encourage the men who are supportive of the women around them who want to obey and do what God has asked them to do. I know from personal observation the persecution that men who are supportive of women in ministry can sometimes endure. I personally want to say thank you to every man who has supported the women around them as they have stepped out to obey God. I applaud those of you who have studied enough to understand that sometimes the purposes of God for women mean that they will minister and perhaps even lead, not because of the ever-changing sway of culture, but because biblically it is the right thing to do.

It is a small percentage of the population, both men and women who are actually called to full-time ministry, but *everyone* has something to do for God. In these last days, we need everyone to find their place and get in it!

Brothers and sisters, we are *not* a threat to each other. We are *not* in competition with each other. We are teammates, both committed to seeing the other succeed and hear, "Well done, thou good and faithful servant!"

The only enemy we have is Satan and the forces of darkness in our world. The only competition we have is Satan and the forces of darkness in our world.

When we understand *why* women exist, *how* God sees us, and *what* He has for us to do, then I trust we will all take our place like Adam and Eve before the fall—standing as one, face to face, hand in hand, ruling and reigning together over Satan and the forces of darkness that have been unleashed on our world.

When I was studying these things for some young women ministers I was working with, the Lord smote my heart when I read the following verses.

He asked her, "Woman, why are you crying? Who is it you are looking for?"

Thinking he was the gardener, she said, "Sir, if you have carried him away, tell me where you have put him, and I will get him."

Jesus said to her, "Mary."

She turned toward him and cried out in Aramaic, "Rabboni!" (which means "Teacher").

Jesus said, "Do not hold on to me, for I have not yet ascended to the Father. Go instead to my brothers and tell them, 'I am ascending to my Father and your Father, to my God and your God.'"

Mary Magdalene went to the disciples with the news: "I have seen the Lord!" And she told them that he had said these things to her (John 20:15-18 NIV).

Mary Magdalene found the disciples and told them, "I have seen the Lord!" Then she gave them his message (John 20:18 NLT).

We looked in Chapter 5 of this book at how within hours of His resurrection, Jesus used Mary to be the first preacher of His resurrection, and He asked her to deliver a message for Him. This is the essence of preaching. God tells you what to say and to whom, and you just deliver His message.

When I read these verses, preparing to minister to these young ladies, the Lord smote my heart and said to me, "Rhonda, just tell them to deliver My messages. Whenever I give them a message, just tell them to deliver My message!"

Just do it. Just deliver His messages, be they to individuals or crowds of tens of thousands. It doesn't matter. Just deliver His messages!

You don't have to get all caught up in titles. Who cares what title they give you or don't give you?

A couple of the ladies in our church were telling me about their grandmother. There was no full gospel church in their area, and so the Lord moved on their grandmother's heart to open her home to start a full gospel church. She led this church, she preached, she won the lost, built the church, she was anointed, and all the people loved her. They even ended up naming the church after her, but they could never bring themselves to call her "pastor." But she did not let that stop her from obeying the Lord!

I am certain that when she got to Heaven, she got the title and the reward that went with it for all of eternity.

This, then, is how you ought to regard us: as servants of Christ and as those entrusted with the mysteries God has revealed. Now it is required that those who have been given a trust must prove faithful. I care very little if I am judged by you or by any human court; indeed, I do not even judge myself. My conscience is clear, but that does not make me innocent. It is the Lord who judges me. Therefore judge nothing before the appointed time; wait until the Lord comes. He will bring to light what is hidden in darkness and will expose the motives of the heart. At that time each will receive their praise from God (1 Corinthians 4:1-5 NIV).

In the end, we will all be seen for exactly who and what we are. Then we will receive our praise from God! That praise, *His* praise, is for eternity!

Women were created to fulfill the will and plan of God! We were not created to be ambitious and just take things into our own hands and make a place for ourselves. No! Like our male counterparts, we are only called to walk with God and do the assignments *He* gives us! May we take our place alongside the great women who went before us, following their legacy of faith and fearless obedience to the Father!

Let's join the ranks of Sarah, Hannah, Rebekah, and others who, in the face of hopeless circumstances, believed God for and received the impossible thing that He had promised. When

Gabriel told Mary the mother of Jesus that she would miraculously conceive a child, she said, "I am the Lord's servant, be it done unto me according to your word!" May that be our response to the miraculous plan of God for *our* lives too, "I am the Lord's servant, be it done unto me according to Your word!" Let's stand with Miriam and Deborah who answered the call of God to lead nations both spiritually and naturally. When moved upon by God, let's preach like Priscilla and prophesy like Huldah. Let's take our place next to the great women of old who fearlessly delivered God's messages, whether to individuals or to crowds of tens of thousands. There is such a legacy of faith and fearless obedience laid out before us that it should inspire us to pick up *our* mantle and take *our* place!

We must be after *His* praise and His praise alone!

I want us to look at one last scripture:

The Lord gave the word: great was the company of those that published it (Psalm 68:11 KJV).

That scripture's meaning is not clear in the King James Version. Let's look at it in the Young's Literal Translation.

*The Lord doth give the saying, The **female proclaimers** [are] a numerous host (Psalm 68:11 YLT).*

Let's look at it in the Amplified Classic.

The Lord gives the word [of power]; the women who bear and publish [the news] are a great host (Psalm 68:11 AMPC).

This is said to be a messianic prophecy, when we see these things happening, a large host of women taking their place and proclaiming His word of power, we know the return of Christ is near.

Wow! How wonderful is that!

Looking over church history, and specifically the great outpourings during this, the church age, we see that women were front and center in almost all, if not all, of the outpourings of God that have occurred.

May it be so in our day too!

APPENDIX A

I am not a Hebrew or Greek scholar, but I do know from my studies that in the Hebrew language there is masculine and feminine gendering in nouns, pronouns, adjectives, verbs and participles, meaning all kinds of words are given masculine or feminine designation when there is nothing masculine or feminine about it. It is that way in other languages too. It is called a grammatical gender system to linguists.

To the non-Hebrew scholar, there doesn't seem to be any clear reason or grammatic rule as to why some words were made masculine and some feminine. Someone just assigned each word a gender when the language was created. I do know Hebrew scholars and linguists acknowledge that it has absolutely nothing to do with gender or something having inherently male or female characteristics. For instance, in the first chapter of Genesis, the word for "water" is a masculine noun, while the word for "dry ground" is a feminine noun. The word *fish* is a feminine noun, and the word *bird* is a masculine noun.

I say all of that to say this: in some versions of the Strong's Exhaustive Concordance, it is notated that the word *aadaam* or Adam is a masculine noun. I did not want that to confuse you into thinking it is referring to *Aadaam* or Adam, the human being, as being someone of the male gender or that the human was masculine. It doesn't mean that at all. It has nothing to do with gender, something being either male or female or inherently masculine or feminine. It is just a quirk of their grammar.

APPENDIX B

I want to take a moment to talk about 1 Corinthians 11:1-16.

Quite honestly, there are *volumes* written about the exact meaning of 1 Corinthians 11:1-16. Scholars and theologians have studied these verses since they were written and have given many different interpretations of these scriptures.

I have intentionally chosen not to address what is written in 1 Corinthians 11 thus far in this book, except as it pertains to women ministering and head coverings. Most scholars believe the rest of these verses are about marriage and the relationship between husbands and wives; therefore, they are outside of the purview of this book.

In an earlier version of this manuscript, I went through these scriptures and talked about them in-depth, but it pulled the manuscript over into marriage. I found myself going further and further on that subject, which took me away from the purpose of this book. I felt like I needed to stay with my subject and stay within the parameters that the Lord gave to me. So I removed that chapter from my book.

But at the same time, I don't want someone using some of these verses in 1 Corinthians 11 wrongly, by taking them outside of their subject in an attempt to argue against what the Bible clearly says about women in other portions of scripture.

So I am just going to say a few things and move on.

I think part of the confusion here is that the King James Version uses the words *man* and *woman* instead of *husband* and *wife*.

Most scholars agree these are marriage verses, but the King James Version is not clear on that.

If you take this outside of marriage and, in verse 3, try to make that word *head* mean "boss and leader," then this scripture gets very convoluted and gets over into what is obviously not scriptural, not sound doctrine, and in direct conflict with the rest of scripture.

If you try to make it say, "the boss and leader of every man is Christ, and the boss and leader of the woman *is* the man, and the boss and leader of Christ *is* God," then none of us humans, neither women nor men, have Father God as *our* boss and leader, only Jesus does. Also, that would make women have neither God the Father nor Jesus as *their* boss and leader, just their husbands. No! Making the word *head* mean "boss and leader" twists that scripture until it becomes *totally* unscriptural and in conflict with the rest of the Bible.

One meaning of the word *head* is "the source." We use it that way regularly in the English language. We might say, for instance, "The head of the river is a natural spring." Meaning, the source of the river is a natural spring of water coming up from the ground.

Actually, most early commentaries on this verse understood that word "head" to mean "the source." So our scripture could be translated, "the source of every man is Christ; and the source of the woman *is* the man; and the source of Christ *is* God." That makes a *lot* more sense and doesn't twist the scripture into bad doctrine.

That actually agrees with John 1:1.

In the beginning was the Word, and the Word was with God, and the Word was God. The same was in the beginning with

God. *All things were made by him; and without him was not any thing made that was made (John 1:1-3 KJV).*

In John 1:2 it says Jesus Himself was the one who made all the things that God spoke and thus He became the source of all creation including Adam (the human) and later the man, Adam.

God is obviously the source of Jesus as God calls him His only begotten Son.

*For God so loved the world, that he gave **his only begotten Son**, that whosoever believeth in him should not perish, but have everlasting life (John 3:16 KJV).*

Adam (the human) was indeed the source of Eve. I don't think Paul saying the *man* is the source of Eve refutes the fact that Adam and Eve were created together in one body as scripture clearly says in Genesis that they were. We need to understand that Paul was making a quick reference to men and women or husbands and wives in Genesis without taking a lot of time to teach in-depth on it.

Let me give you an example that might help our understanding. If I took some raw milk from a cow and I churned and churned that raw milk, it would eventually separate the butter from what was now left of the milk (buttermilk) in the churn. If someone walked up and asked me where I got the butter from, it would not be improper to say, "It came out of this buttermilk." That would not be an inaccurate statement, nor would it refute that the butter and the buttermilk used to be together as raw milk. Does that make sense?

In the same way, Paul saying "the man" was the source of Eve is not an inaccurate statement and does not refute that they were together in one body before they were separated by God.

So, interpreting that word *head* as "the source" instead of as "the boss or leader" is in complete harmony with the rest of the scripture, and it in no way diminishes the worth and value of the woman.

I don't believe that Paul saying women (wives) are the glory of the men (husbands) is diminishing to a woman at all, especially when you realize that the word *glory* here means "what evokes good opinion, i.e. something that has inherent intrinsic worth," like it is used in the temptation of Christ.

*Again, the devil taketh him up into an exceeding high mountain, and sheweth him all the kingdoms of the world, **and the glory of them** (Matthew 4:8 KJV).*

I don't believe Paul saying, in verses 8 and 9 of 1 Corinthians 11, *"man is not of the woman; but the woman of the man. Neither was the man created for the woman; but the woman for the man"* in any way refutes that they were created together in the same body at the beginning (like the butter coming from the buttermilk in our earlier example). In fact, he goes on then to talk about the interdependence of husbands and wives (men and women).

Again, most scholars believe this chapter is about husbands and wives, but because the King James Version doesn't translate it that way, I didn't want to cause confusion by failing to address it.

ABOUT RHONDA GARVER

Rhonda Garver began her ministry as a missionary in Asia, where she served until the Lord joined her with her husband, Mark Garver. Together, the couple co-pastors Cornerstone Word of Life Church in Madison, Alabama, and leads its Bible Institute and School of Ministry. Known for her strong teaching gift, Rhonda frequently ministers nationally and internationally and hosts Women in Ministry Convocations around the world.

In the Right Hands, This Book Will Change Lives!

Most of the people who need this message will not be looking for this book. To change their lives, you need to **put a copy of this book in their hands.**

Our ministry is constantly seeking methods to find the people who need this anointed message to change their lives. **Will you help us reach these people?**

Extend this ministry by sowing three, five, ten, or *even more* books today and change people's lives for the better! Your generosity will be part of catalyzing the Great Awakening that many have been prophesying and praying for.

YOUR HOUSE OF
FAITH

Sign up for a **FREE** subscription to the Harrison House digital magazine and get excellent content delivered directly to your inbox!

harrisonhouse.com/signup

Sign up for Messages that Equip You to Walk in the Abundant Life

• Receive biblically sound and Spirit-filled encouragement to focus on and maintain your faith
• Grow in faith through biblical teachings, prayers, and other spiritual insights
• Connect with a community of believers who share you values and beliefs

perience Fresh Teachings and piration to Build Your Faith

epen your understanding of God's purpose for life
y connected and inspired on your faith journey
arn how to grow spiritually in your walk with God